*Longman Study Texts*

# Doctor Faustus

**Longman Study Texts**
General editor: Richard Adams

*Titles in the series*

Jane Austen
  *Emma*
  *Pride and Prejudice*
Charlotte Brontë
  *Jane Eyre*
Emily Brontë
  *Wuthering Heights*
Charles Dickens
  *Great Expectations*
  *Oliver Twist*
George Eliot
  *Silas Marner*
  *The Mill on the Floss*
Thomas Hardy
  *The Mayor of Casterbridge*
Aldous Huxley
  *Brave New World*
D H Lawrence
  *Sons and Lovers*
George Orwell
  *Animal Farm*
  *Nineteen Eighty-Four*
Paul Scott
  *Staying On*
Virginia Woolf
  *To the Lighthouse*
Oliver Goldsmith
  *She Stoops to Conquer*
Nadine Gordimer
  *July's People*
Ben Jonson
  *Volpone*
Christopher Marlowe
  *Doctor Faustus*
Somerset Maugham
  *Short Stories*
Alan Paton
  *Cry, the Beloved Country*

Terence Rattigan
  *The Winslow Boy*
Willy Russell
  *Educating Rita*
Peter Shaffer
  *Amadeus*
  *Equus*
  *The Royal Hunt of the Sun*
William Shakespeare
  *Macbeth*
  *The Merchant of Venice*
  *Romeo and Juliet*
Richard Brinsley Sheridan
  *The Rivals*
  *The School for Scandal*
John Webster
  *The White Devil*
  *The Duchess of Malfi*
Bernard Shaw
  *Androcles and the Lion*
  *Arms and the Man*
  *Caesar and Cleopatra*
  *The Devil's Disciple*
  *Major Barbara*
  *Pygmalion*
  *St Joan*
H G Wells
  *The History of Mr Polly*
Oscar Wilde
  *The Importance of Being Earnest*
Robin Jenkins
  *The Cone-Gatherers*
J B Priestley
  *An Inspector Calls*
Editor: George MacBeth
  *Poetry for Today*
Editor: Michael Marland
  *Short Stories for Today*

# Christopher Marlowe

# **Doctor Faustus**

*edited by*
**Linda Cookson**

*with a personal essay by*
**Jan Kott**

LONGMAN GROUP UK LIMITED
*Longman House,*
*Burnt Mill, Harlow, Essex CM20 2JE, England*
*and Associated Companies throughout the world.*

First published 1984
Third impression 1987

*Set in 10/12pt. Linotron 202 Baskerville*
*Produced by Longman Group (FE) Ltd.*
**Printed in Hong Kong**

ISBN 0-582-35390-4

# Contents

*A personal essay by Jan Kott*                                    vi

'The Faustus Figure in Life and Legend'
   I  The shapes of Evil: a variety of devils         vi
  II  Living legends: the men behind the myth          viii
 III  Despair, Repentance, Damnation                    xiii


*Introduction*                                                   xviii

'Profit and delight': Marlowe and his age                        xviii
'Cut is the branch': Faustus as tragic hero                      xxi
The writing of *Doctor Faustus*                                  xxvi
The text of *Doctor Faustus*                                     xxvii


*Doctor Faustus* (*text and notes*)                              1

*Study questions*                                                148

# A personal essay by Jan Kott

## The Faustus Figure in Life and Legend

### I The shapes of Evil: a variety of devils

On the title page of the 1616 edition of *The Tragical History of the Life and the Death of Doctor Faustus*, Faustus is standing in his Wittenberg study, wearing a cape and a solemn gown lined with fur, most probably of sable. In his left hand he is holding a book; in his right, a wand with which he has drawn a circle of magical signs on the floor. In Shakespeare's *The Tempest*, Prospero drew circles in the sand with the same magical staff, when on his desert island, and he read incantations from a book of mystic knowledge to summon the Airy Spirit, Ariel. Faustus also uses a book to summon spirits, but in Marlowe's play, the spirit is a devil (Act I, Scene I, lines 47–49):

> Divinity, adieu!
> These metaphysics of magicians
> And necromantic books are heavenly.

The very same 1616 title page also shows the devil proffering a hairy paw to Faustus. Depicted as a dragon, he has black wings, a curled tail and a goatee. But Marlowe realized that the play's main actor next to Faustus must appear on stage in human form and this explains Faustus's command (Act I, Scene III, lines 23–26):

> I charge thee to return and change thy shape;
> Thou art too ugly to attend on me.
> Go, and return an old Franciscan friar;
> That holy shape becomes a devil best.

In the folklore of virtually all nations, there are stories about a man who sells his soul to the devil, and who signs a writ with his own blood. Faustus must also sign a contract with his own blood. And when out of horror his blood congeals, the resourceful devil sends for a 'chafer of fire' to make the blood flow again. The ceremony is that of the folktale, but both the devil and the man in Marlowe's play are far removed from their traditional counterparts.

The man who sold his soul to the devil is a 'conjuror laureate', Doctor of Theology, tutor of 'the flowering pride of Wittenberg'. Wittenberg was one of the great Renaissance centres of learning, and later, of course, of Protestant orthodoxy. It is apparent that the Mephostophilis who appears in Faustus's university study at Wittenberg is akin to the devil who attempted to dispute with Luther, that very architect of Protestantism in Germany. At Wartburg Castle, one can still see the stain from the inkwell that Luther is said to have hurled at the fiend. He supposedly appeared before Luther as 'a grey monk', like Mephostophilis in *Doctor Faustus*. Marlowe, after Luther, modernized and reactivated the mediaeval devil and endowed him with new intellectual powers. Mephostophilis is a sophisticated devil and knows his adversary's theology by heart. Far from triumphing over him, Faustus, the Renaissance scholar, sells the Lutheran devil his soul for power and knowledge. Luther would never have made such a mistake. He writes: 'Does not witchcraft, then, merit death, which is a revolt of the creature against the creator, a denial to God of the authority it accords to the demon?'

Marlowe's most astonishing idea was to set Faustus's tragical history within the frame of a mediaeval morality play. In the well-known morality play *The Castle of Perseverance* (c. 1425), the sinner, like Faustus, meets the Seven Deadly Sins on his way from the cradle to the grave, while Good and Bad Angels fight for his soul. But in *Doctor Faustus*, the Seven Deadly Sins are but a grotesque horror show performed by devils for Faustus's delight, while the Bad Angel seems far more convincing than the Good one. Almost all morality plays end, like *Everyman* (c. 1495), with the sinner's repentance at the moment of death. But Faustus does not repent: 'This night I conjure, though I die therefor'. Faustus dies condemned.

## II Living legends: the men behind the myth

The literary and legendary prototype of Faustus was born around 1480 in Kündlingen, in Germany. He was not yet thirty when his daring and magic made him widely renowned. He presented himself as Magister Georgius Sabellicus, Faustus junior, 'fountain of necromancers, astrologer, *magus secundus*, chiromancer, aeromancer, pyromancer, second in hydromancy'. He must have gained considerable acclaim as an astrologer, since, for a horoscope, he charged the German princes ten gulden, the price of a horse. To summon the dead as a necromancer, Faustus cast shadows with a magic lantern and thus must have been knowledgeable in optics. He wandered all over Germany, from one university town to the next, through Heidelberg, Nuremberg, Erfurt, Basel and Worms. He even made his way as far as Cracow, where he was said to have studied and taught a secret science. But he remained the longest in Wittenberg, and it was in Wittenberg that Hamlet received his education. Dare we imagine, with historical license in hand, that Faustus drank wine with Hamlet in the taverns of Wittenberg and taught him how necromancers summon ghosts?! Faustus died in 1540 or 1541 in Freiburg, when, during an experiment, his chemicals suddenly exploded. This first Faustus, like all his literary successors, fell victim to his untamed intellectual curiosity.

Faustus must have quickly become a legendary figure, as less than fifty years after his death *The Historie of the damnable life and deserved death of Doctor John Faustus* was published in Frankfurt on the river Main and was translated into English as early as 1592.

The German Faust book was didactic in purpose, aiming to warn against wicked practices and pacts with impure powers.

And yet it is highly astonishing that already in this naïve and moralistic story the Faustus figure arouses not only horror and disgust, but also fascination:

> ... he studied day and night therein: in so much that he could not abide to be called Doktor of Divinity, but waxed a worldly man, and himself an Astrologian, and a Mathematician: and for a shadow sometimes a Physician, and did great cures, namely, with herbs, roots, water, drinks, receipts, and clysters.

The first Faustus, the real one, a provincial magician, a charlatan and clandestine teacher of illicit arts, lived during a great epoch. Besides Paracelsus, among his contemporaries were Copernicus, Columbus and Leonardo da Vinci. Reflected in the Faustus legend and myth is the brilliance and courage of his contemporaries. For Renaissance man, even a pact with the devil was not too high a price to pay for knowledge and power over the world. Already in *The Historie of the damnable life*, the first provision in Faustus's pact with Mephostophilis had guaranteed that 'The spirit should tell him nothing but that which is true'. The devil is not allowed to lie. And this intensified both the fascination and the horror aroused by the infernal pact. 'A sound magician is a demi-god,' exclaims Marlowe's Faustus in his Wittenberg study. 'Here try thy brains to get a deity!'

In no other Renaissance text is the fascination with secret knowledge and the horror of devil worship more apparent than in Pico della Mirandola's famous *Oration on the Dignity of Man*, written in 1486, when the first German Faustus was not much more than five years old.

> ... magic has two forms, one of which depends entirely on the work and authority of demons, a thing to be abhorred, so help me God of truth, and a monstrous thing. The other, when it rightly pursued, is nothing else than the utter

perfection of natural philosophy ... The former not only the Christian religion but all religions and every well-constituted state condemn and abhor. The latter all wise men, all peoples devoted to the study of heavenly and divine things, approve and embrace ...

Denouncing demonology and recanting magic did not protect Mirandola from charges of heresy. In his *Oration*, he had defended too openly the dignity of the magus and the whole tradition of hermetic (or mystic) science, from Greek Mysteries and Gnosis to Persian magi and mediaeval sorcerers. The distinction between white and black magic, between scientific speculation and magical conjurations, was far from clear. In the experiments and speculations of even the most eminent scholars, the dividing line between astronomy and astrology, chemistry and alchemy, logic and cabalistic magic, science and science fiction remained blurred, almost until the end of the seventeenth century.

John Dee, a mathematician and an astronomer, was the most 'Faustian' figure in Elizabethan and Jacobean England. Born in 1527, while the German Faustus was alive, he died in 1608, four years after the first posthumous edition of Marlowe's *Doctor Faustus*. Dee had left behind him two extraordinary works. The first was his introduction to the English translation of Euclid, '... where also are disclosed', as the title page of the 1570 edition announces, 'certaine new Secrets Mathematicall and Mechanicall, until these our daies gratly missed'. Dee's introduction continues to loom large in the history of English mathematics: it is the first demonstration of the applicability of mathematics to mechanics. Unpublished until half a century after his death, Dee's second work, *A True and faithful Relation of what passed for many years between Dr John Dee ... and some spirits*, bears the Faustian stamp. The book bristles with the signs of the zodiac, Hebraic and Arabic letters, and numerical conjurations used to summon spirits. On the floor of his Wittenberg study, Marlowe's Faustus draws similar figures

(Act I, Scene III, lines 8–13):

> Within this circle is Jehovah's name
> Forward and backward anagrammatiz'd,
> The breviated names of holy saints,
> Figures of every adjunct to the heavens,
> And characters of signs and erring stars,
> By which the spirits are enforc'd to rise.

Numerical conjurations have also been discovered in Newton's manuscripts. Mystical speculation has accompanied astrology for centuries, representing perhaps the pre-scientific intuition that creation, matter and movement are a mathematical formula. Yet according to hearsay, Dee was a conjuror. In 1583, afraid perhaps that he would be indicted for witchcraft, he left England for Poland where he lived for several years. After his departure, a fanatical mob charged into his house in Mortlake, plundered his library and destroyed his collection of scientific instruments. Marlowe could not but have heard of Dee. At the time he was completing his studies at Corpus Christi College in Cambridge.

The library in Mortlake was one of the finest among Renaissance book collections. Fortunately, the catalogue has survived. Dee had owned the original edition of Copernicus's *Revolutiones* from 1543, Albrecht Dürer's *De symmetria humani corporis*, and Vitruvius's treatise *De architectura*, which influenced the design of Renaissance theatres. But Dee's library also contained a surprisingly exhaustive collection of hermetic books and magical manuscripts, including works by Roger Bacon and Cornelius Agrippa. Marlowe's Faustus mentions the 'wise Bacon' and compares himself to Agrippa (Act I, Scene I, lines 111–117):

> And I ...
> Will be as cunning as Agrippa was,
> Whose shadows made all Europe honour him.

Roger Bacon was a thirteenth-century magician who constructed the famous 'talking' brazen head, regarded as a demonic invention. Bacon was probably an excellent hydromancer as he used steam and streams of water to produce sounds. The German Faustus presented himself, let us recall, as 'pyromancer, second in hydromancy'.

Cornelius Agrippa (1486–1535) was the contemporary of the German Faustus. They could easily have met at one of the German universities which Faustus visited. Or even at Wittenberg. Perhaps Marlowe had Cornelius Agrippa in mind when he gave the name of Cornelius to one of the two 'conjurors', 'infamous through the world', who lure Faustus (Act I, Scene I, lines 135–139).

> The miracles that magic will perform
> Will make thee vow to study nothing else.
> He that is grounded in astrology,
> Enrich'd with tongues, well seen in minerals,
> Hath all the principles magic doth require.

This is how Marlowe's Cornelius addresses Faustus.

In the English translation of *The damnable life* Faustus is called 'the insatiable Speculator'. In Marlowe, he conjures spirits to 'resolve me of all ambiguities'. Leonardo da Vinci drew models of airships, flawlessly calculating their aerodynamic properties. But they could not rise into the air as there was no energy to propel them, and no metals light enough to enable man to fly with Leonardo's wings.

In the prologue to Marlowe's play, the chorus compares Faustus to Icarus who soared in the sky on wings kneaded from wax. The wings melted in the sun. Icarus crashed (Prologue, lines 21–22):

> His waxen wings did mount above his reach,
> And melting, heavens conspir'd his overthrow.

## III Despair, Repentance, Damnation

Faustus believes in demons, or at least in their might, otherwise he would not summon them. Yet he does not believe in hell. After death, he speculates, he will go to Elysium to join the sages of ancient times: 'I think hell's a fable.' But Mephostophilis is a more skilful dialectician than Faustus. He does not talk of fire and brimstone or carry a pitchfork. Look at me, he says to Faustus, hell is where I am (Act II, Scene I, lines 120–125):

> Hell hath no limits, nor is circumscrib'd
> In one self place, but where we are is hell,
> And where hell is, there must we ever be;
> And, to be short, when all the world dissolves
> And every creature shall be purify'd,
> And places shall be hell that is not heaven.

Marlowe's Mephostophilis is a tormented spirit, almost tragic, like Milton's Satan: Mephostophilis, Lucifer and Beelzebub are fallen angels whose endless torture is their separation from God. They tempt in order not to be alone in their misery. A metaphysical seriousness, foreshadowing Donne, unexpectedly surfaces in Mephostophilis's dialogue with Faustus (Act II, Scene I, lines 43–44):

FAUSTUS Why, have you any pain that torture other?
MEPHOSTOPHILIS As great as have the human souls of men.

The drama of the Renaissance scholar, which begins and ends in his university study, takes place between heaven and hell. The Renaissance choice between a science constrained by dogma and a crude technology, and magic that promises power over the world, becomes the Christian choice between damnation and salvation. 'This word damnation terrifies not him' – but Faustus has not yet signed his soul away. Afterwards he knows: 'Faustus, thou art damned'. *The Historie of the damnable Life* ... was changed by Marlowe to *The Tragical History of the Life and the Death*: still, the words 'damned' and 'damnation' reappear constantly in his drama: 'damned art', 'damned perpetually', 'damned soul'. In the last soliloquy, just before midnight strikes, Faustus will say once again, 'Oh, no end is limited to damned souls'. Disbelief in God's compassion is the gravest sin against the Holy Spirit in Christian theology (Act II, Scene II, lines 12–13):

GOOD ANGEL  Faustus, repent; yet God will pity thee.
BAD ANGEL  Thou are a spirit; God cannot pity thee.

In mediaeval morality plays, in *Everyman*, in *Mankind*, in *The Castle of Perseverance*, man sins, but at the last moment, as Death leads him to the grave, he regrets his sins and is saved. Faustus does not repent and is therefore damned. He has known from the beginning that his damnation is inevitable and that there is no cure for it. His human greatness is his refusal to repent. 'To God? He loves thee not.' Faustus rejects God who rejected Faustus. He receives his damnation with pride, perhaps even with a kind of morose relish. 'That is blasphemy', says the Good Angel to Faustus. But the transgression is temptation. Not even the taboo will stop the Renaissance Faustus. His angel, not unlike the angel of modern science, is the angel of evil (Act I, Scene I, lines 73–76):

Go forward, Faustus, in that famous art
Wherein all nature's treasure is contain'd.
Be thou on earth as Jove is in the sky,
Lord and commander of these elements.

This Faustus resembles the other mythical hero of post-classical theatre, Don Juan, who knows that joy is knowledge and that the price of such knowledge is hell. He also knows that joy is often a sacrilege. He defies Heaven every time he leads another of his thousand women to the altar. Donna

Elvira is a nun, Christ's bride, and marriage with her is sacrilege. Don Juan dares God in whom he does not believe. Yet God accepts the Don's challenge. Don Juan meets his end, like Faustus, in thunder and lightning. Friends find Faustus lying face downwards and his limbs 'all torn asunder by the hand of death'. Don Juan disappears into the bowels of the earth.

In Thomas Kyd's *Spanish Tragedy*, staged in 1592, the same year as *Doctor Faustus*, the hero tells of 'monstrous times' when 'the soul delights in interdicted things'. Faustus and Don Juan know both by senses and by intellect the delight of transgression. The great teacher of this delight is Lucifer. He discloses a truth, one which twentieth-century literature will repeatedly rediscover: 'But Faustus, in hell is all manner of delight.' Marlowe himself must have been acquainted with this truth, as Faustus's lines have a personal tone that is not found in any of his other plays, nor even perhaps in any of Shakespeare's dramas, except for *The Tempest*. In a strange way, Marlowe's Faustus from the end of the Renaissance, who so well knows hell to be the price of joy and knowledge, is toward the end of the twentieth century, our contemporary (Act V, Scene I, lines 101–105):

> Sweet Helen, make me immortal with a kiss.
> Her lips suck forth my soul: see where it flies.
> Come, Helen, come, give me my soul again.
> Here will I dwell, for heaven is in these lips,
> And all is dross that is not Helena.

All that is not heaven will be hell, Mephostophilis tells Faustus. All that is not Helen is nothingness, but the Helen offered to Faustus is an apparition. And he knows it: 'These are but shadows, not substantial'. Heaven is in Helen's lips, yet she herself is the gift of Hell. Her celestial lips 'suck forth' the soul, as the infernal succuba. A kiss from Helen imparts immortality, but in this Christian anti-morality play, Faustus's only immortality is his eternal death and damnation (Act V, Scene II, lines 179–182):

all beasts are happy,
For when they die
Their souls are soon dissolv'd in elements;
But mine must live still to be plagu'd in hell.

Marlowe's *Doctor Faustus* is in essence a tragedy of despair. The words 'despair' and 'desperate' recur thirteen times. 'Desperate' are Faustus's thoughts, 'desperate' is his 'enterprise', and 'desperate' his 'lunacy'. 'Damned art thou, Faustus, damned – despair and die!' But why does this Christian despair move us even though we do not believe? Faustus's despair, Marlowe's own despair, is the despair of disbelievers. It is despair because knowledge is useless: death is inevitable, and the world cannot be changed.

'I'll burn my books!' These are Faustus's last words. The other great conjuror, Prospero, from Shakespeare's *The Tempest*, also renounces 'rough magic':

I'll break my staff,
Bury it certain fathoms in the earth,
And deeper than did ever plummet sound
I'll drown my book.

In *Doctor Faustus* and in *The Tempest*, in the beginning and the end of the greatest period in post-classical theatre, we find a backdrop of despair. Prospero concludes his epilogue: 'And my ending is despair, / Unless I be relieved by prayer'. But Faustus says: 'I do repent and yet I do despair.'

Despair is loss of hope. 'Despair' – in Latin *de-sperare* – comes from 'sperare', to hope. The despair of the late Renaissance was loss of hope in the power of human reason to transform the world and human nature, loss of illusions about the greatness and beauty of man. At the peak of Renaissance optimism, Pico della Mirandola wrote in his *Oration on the Dignity of Man*:

At last it seems to me I have come to understand why man is the most fortunate of creatures and consequently worthy of all admiration and what precisely is that rank which is his lot in the universal Chain of Being – a rank to be envied not only by brutes but even by the stars and by minds beyond this world. It is a matter of past faith and a wondrous one. Why should it not be? For it is on this very account that man is rightly called and judged a great miracle and a wonderful creature indeed.

In 1601, Hamlet will repeat after Mirandola:

What a piece of work is a man, how noble in reason, how infinite in faculties, in form and moving, how express and admirable in action, how like an angel in apprehension, how like a god: the beauty of the world; the paragon of the animals . . .

But Hamlet's praise of beauty and human dignity will have a bitter conclusion: 'And yet to me, what is this quintessence of dust? Man delights not me.'

Marlowe was already dead. On the evening of 30 May 1593 at a Deptford tavern, he was stabbed in the brow, 'over his right eye'. He lay like Faustus, face to the floor. The murderer was pardoned. Notorious as an atheist and blasphemer, Marlowe was entangled in a number of squalid affairs. His murder was probably an execution.

Only seven years later, in 1600, a pamphlet will proclaim Marlowe's death, like Faustus's, to have been an act of divine judgement: 'Thus did God, the true executioner of divine justice, invoke the end of an impious atheist.'

*Translated by* Michael Kott
Deniz Firincioglu

# Introduction

## 'Profit and delight': Marlowe and his age

Christopher Marlowe was a child of the Renaissance. He was born in 1564 – the same year as both Shakespeare and Galileo. And, like Faustus himself, he was born into a unique and exhilarating 'new' age that offered endless possibilities for advancement, even to a son 'of parents base of stock'. The Renaissance was a time of excitement, of exploration and of constant questioning; a time of heady intoxication with travel, with learning and with discovery; and a time in which beauty, the senses, and the very potential of man himself, were celebrated lovingly in verbal and visual splendour. It was an age that allowed young Christopher Marlowe, son of a Canterbury shoemaker, to win a scholarship to Cambridge and become an admired associate of famous intellectual thinkers. And it was an age in which the study of humble John Faustus could become the academic hive of the entire 'flowering pride of Wittenberg'.

Faustus embodies, in many ways, the very essence of Renaissance man, greatly gifted and aspiring always towards further greatness. This was the famous era of cartography – Christopher Columbus had discovered America; the globe had been circumnavigated by intrepid explorers. And Faustus's speeches reflect all the wonder and delight in contemplating man's extended horizons that was characteristic of the Elizabethans. He is lured by Valdes' travellers' tales of 'Indian Moors' and 'Lapland giants'. Not only does he formulate eager plans to send spirit emissaries to 'search all corners of the new-found world', but he himself undertakes a breathtaking Grand Tour of Europe. He crosses from Trier to Rome, marvelling both at nature's bounty and at the architectural magnificence wrought by man. And these descriptions are studded with references to precious metals – especially to gold, which is evoked as a rich and resplendent symbol of human wealth and ingenuity. At Venice, for example, the focus centres on the dazzling splendour of St Mark's, a 'sumptuous temple' (Act III, Scene I, lines 19–20):

Whose frame is pav'd with sundry colour'd stones
And roof'd aloft with curious work in gold.

Both the depths and the heights of the created world intrigue Faustus. He dreams of the 'orient pearl' that rests on the bed of the ocean. Conversely, his thoughts soar constantly to the stars in the sky, which are a zone of perpetual fascination for him, just as they were for the very first astronomers. To Faustus, they signify both infinity – 'Had I as many souls as there be stars,' he sighs – and supernatural beauty. Helen, for example, is 'clad in the beauty of a thousand stars'. But perhaps more mysteriously still, they signify the key to a hidden secret. His interrogation of Mephostophilis about the 'celestial bodies' is urgent and keen. For it leads to the most important – and unanswerable – question of all (Act II, Scene II, line 69):

Now tell me who made the world.

Religious inquiry was an issue central to Renaissance man, for the authority of the Church – which had been so absolute in the Middle Ages – was now lessening significantly. The Reformation, for example, had cast doubts upon the necessity of religious conformity. And contemporary thought was beginning to place the responsibility for personal salvation onto separate individuals, rather than onto the Church as a corporate institution. Marlowe himself was clearly impatient with the rigours of the old order, and attracted by the possibilities of unorthodoxy. When living in London, for instance, he was a member of a group of intellectuals known as the 'School of Night', who challenged conventional Christian doctrines. And although *Doctor Faustus* ultimately follows and reinforces the moral framework of a conventional mediaeval Morality play – in which allegorical figures contend for the hero's soul – it nevertheless also gives

dynamic expression to a whole series of extraordinarily provoca-
tive theories.

The seductive charm of Humanist thought, which focused on
Man as the centre of creation, is voiced very alluringly by
Mephostophilis (Act II, Scene II, lines 5–7):

> But think'st thou heaven is such a glorious thing?
> I tell thee, Faustus, it is not half so fair
> As thou or any man that breathes on earth.

The convention of marriage is challenged with vigour and contempt ('Marriage is but a ceremonial toy'). There is spirited and
incisive satire of the Church's rituals and officials. Mephostophilis is instructed to return in the form of 'an old Franciscan
friar' because 'that holy shape becomes a devil best'. The Pope
is presented as a humourless megalomaniac, void of compassion, or even of commonsense. And although the final vision of
hell displays all the lurid horror of a mediaeval painting, it was
earlier evoked for us – with simple and unforgettable profundity –
as a terrifying metaphysical conundrum. 'Why, this is hell,'
explained Mephostophilis in answer to Faustus's question, 'nor
am I out of it.'

The Renaissance was an age for living dangerously, an age for
what the poet Spenser described as 'daring-do'. Its climate of
glamour and excitement inspired a spirit of heroism and rebellion. Yet the traditions of the Middle Ages still weighed heavily
and were massed in grim readiness to crush the over-
presumptuous. Ultimately, it was an age for people who were
prepared to take risks – both physically and intellectually. And
Christopher Marlowe was a notorious risk-taker. It is known,
for example, that – even as a university student – he spent some
time in France as a secret agent. Moreover, his obstinate
defiance of established patterns of thought and behaviour led to
charges of atheism, blasphemy and homosexuality being prepared against him by his political enemies.

In Marlowe's personal life, this constant involvement in forbidden and hazardous activities was eventually to breed disaster: at the age of only twenty nine he was murdered, in highly suspicious circumstances, during a brawl at an inn. But in the context of his career as a dramatist, it yielded – in *Doctor Faustus* – an artistic achievement of unique and triumphant stature. For it is a play that dramatizes with intense poignancy a dilemma of which Marlowe himself was only too aware: the dilemma of a man trapped between two worlds. A brave new world 'of profit and delight' had been found. But what had been the cost?

## 'Cut is the branch': Faustus as tragic hero

Like Icarus in his flight across the heavens, Doctor Faustus challenges the infinite: he seeks control of a space and medium that are not rightfully his. His longing for personal immortality and for a limitless empire that 'stretcheth as far as doth the mind of man' is an arrogant rejection of all earthly constraints of time and place. And his magic draws him deeper and deeper into these forbidden dimensions. He conjures up spirits of the heroic past and superimposes them onto the contemporary mortal world; he soars skyward in a chariot drawn by dragons to view 'the clouds, the planets and the stars'.

Such defiance is in vain, however, as Marlowe demonstrates with painful clarity. For the supernatural cannot be confounded by a mere illusionist. And as surely as the wax melted from Icarus's artificial wings, so Faustus's imagined powers dissolve, and he is returned to the physical reality of his study and of human time. Despite all his aspirations to the contrary, he remains earthbound: he is still 'but Faustus, and a man'. The failure of his attempt to transcend this limitation was as inevitable as the continued striking of the clock (Act V, Scene II, lines 146–147):

> The stars move still, time runs, the clock will strike,
> The devil will come, and Faustus must be damn'd.

And this is not only his tragedy, but perhaps also our own.

Traditionally, tragedy moves its audience to experience both pity and terror, and *Doctor Faustus* is no exception. Faustus falls, like Lucifer before him, because of his 'aspiring pride and insolence'. It was pride that led him to consider himself superhuman, and to glory in the belief that (Act I, Scene I, line 61):

A sound magician is a demi-god.

It is pride that makes him remain 'resolute' in resisting the mercy of God, even in the face of certain death and the 'perpetual' tortures of hell. He is, the Chorus directs us, a being distended with pride: a repulsive and deformed creature 'swollen with cunning of a self-conceit'. Yet when the second Scholar makes the gruesome discovery of the corpse's 'mangled limbs', his cry – 'O help us, heaven!' – is a cry of compassion for a man, not a monster. Moreover, it is not merely a cry for one man only: it is a cry for all mankind. Faustus's fate has become an emblem of both the 'pity' and the 'terror' of our own predicament.

*Doctor Faustus* is a play founded on oppositions, as is confirmed by the curious symmetry of the characters and events within it. The action ranges from high seriousness to comedy, encompassing the realms of both heaven and hell. Characters can be paired morally – there are good and bad scholars as well as good and bad angels, for instance – or coupled within specific relationships, such as that between master and servant. Thus, it is a play in which all the extremes and contradictory impulses that form part of human experience are contrasted and balanced. And nowhere is this duality of approach more apparent than in the presentation of Faustus himself, who unites within his single personality mankind's potential both for good and for evil. At his greatest, he typifies the qualities of imagination and courage that reflect man at his most magnificent. Yet at his worst, he demonstrates a stupidity and a moral grossness that make him far inferior even to the 'brutish beast' that he longs, at the end of his life, to become.

Faustus's weaknesses are many. His childish preoccupation with trivia and theatricality, for instance, which is apparent from the very beginning of the play in his enthusiasm for complicated spells and elaborate chalk circles, is to corrode his intelligence at several crucial points. Constantly, for example, he is won from thoughts of repentance by mere spectacle, responding with uncritical delight to the bizarre sequence of diabolical cabaret acts that are performed in his study. A macabre dance routine by crown-carrying devils enchants him so powerfully that God is forgotten. He is distracted from thoughts of marriage by the cheap joke of a devil in drag. His response to the seedy talent parade presented by the Seven Deadly Sins is one of ill-judged rapture (Act II, Scene II, line 173):

O, how this sight doth delight my soul!

And eventually, of course, this trait within his character is to provide an index of his moral and intellectual degeneration. For it is one of the central ironies of *Doctor Faustus* that the man who aspired to 'wall all Germany with brass', to re-route mighty rivers and to build a bridge 'through the moving air' should squander his magical powers on a succession of ridiculous practical jokes involving ear-boxing, false legs and a straw head.

Faustus's disconcerting capacity for small-mindedness is also apparent on two other – more sinister – levels. Firstly, we can observe alarming weaknesses in his arguments and convictions. For despite his famed skill as a debater – at the peak of his career he could make entire universities 'ring with *sic probo*' – he proves unequal to the subject he is attempting to master. Ignoring clear signs, for instance, that Mephostophilis is a terrifyingly powerful intelligence, who is perfectly able to make intellectual (and literal!) mincemeat out of him, he persists in patronizing the devil with lofty and misconceived advice that he should 'learn . . . of Faustus manly fortitude'. And despite haunting descriptions of the wretched and 'unhappy souls' who are 'deprived of everlasting bliss', he persists stubbornly in his determinedly heroic and oddly unimaginative view of hell (Act II, Scene I, lines 137–138):

> Nay, and this be hell, I'll willingly be damn'd:
> What, sleeping, eating, walking, and disputing!

The second way in which Faustus's human small-mindedness is shown to be dangerous and destructive is dramatized vividly towards the end of the play. For knowledge and power have failed to expand his horizons beyond his single self. Rather, he has become a mere pleasure-seeker, intent on his own personal gratification. This, the Bad Angel reminds us, is a fatal error, for (Act V, Scene II, line 133):

> He that loves pleasure must for pleasure fall.

And Faustus's final degradation – his passion for the devil representing Helen of Troy – confirms the debasement and vain futility of the pleasure principle. When Faustus exits with Helen to consummate his lust in an act that can be only a hollow sham ('make me immortal with a kiss' is spoken, after all, by a man with only minutes of stage time left to live), his commitment to evil has become total. And the Old Man now knows that there is nothing further he can do to save him.

Faustus, like most Elizabethan tragic heroes, is ultimately responsible for his own fate. But significantly, this does not preclude our feeling sympathy for him. We can sympathize with him in his loneliness, for example. For as his life draws to its close, we can see that it is Faustus himself – rather than any of the 'low' characters – who is the real clown of the play: the magic is over; the admiring crowds are all gone; and he is left alone on the stage, with only his 'sad thoughts' as companions. Moreover, we can also sympathize with him – at least to some extent – as the bewildered victim of a calculated deception. His 'overthrow' was after all, as the Chorus told us, 'conspir'd'. And, as Mephostophilis gleefully confirms, Faustus's original act of rebellion against God was entered upon less freely than he could ever have imagined. The prankster and conjuror has been himself the butt of a cruel practical joke (Act V, Scene II, lines 95–99):

I do confess it, Faustus, and rejoice.
'Twas I that, when thou wert i' the way to heaven,
Damn'd up thy passage; when thou took'st the book
To view the scriptures, then I turn'd the leaves
And led thine eye.

Finally, however, it is Faustus's own uncompromising courage in the face of the destiny he has forged for himself that most commands our sympathy. Even at the beginning of the play there was an impressive and heroic resonance in his rhetoric. However misplaced his self-confidence, the defiance of ringing cries such as 'This night I'll conjure though I die therefor' and 'This word "damnation" terrifies not him' was magnetic and appealing. And this desperate heroic grandeur is sustained to the very end of his life. Although Faustus's determination to be 'resolute' amounts to a stubbornness that is merely foolhardy, it still expresses – within its own terms – a bravery of spirit that is noble and almost admirable. Like Shakespeare's Macbeth, he commands our respect as well as our pity in his deliberate decision to continue in a life of evil, even against the voice of his own conscience. And, like the heroes of all the great tragedies, he comes – albeit only partially – to a fuller and wiser perception of the order of the universe, and to a deeper, although painful, understanding of himself. As the clock strikes twelve, for example, he knows only too clearly whom he should blame for his plight: 'No, Faustus, curse thyself.' Yet he will neither ask for mercy nor try to evade execution. And significantly (unlike most other tragic heroes) he has destroyed no one but himself.

In common with almost all of mankind, Faustus is fascinated by fire, and mesmerized by the power and danger that it represents. He heats blood on a chafer of fire from hell; he travels in a 'chariot burning bright'; made invisible by 'Pluto's blue fire', he scatters squibs in the Vatican; and the face of Helen – which 'burnt the topless towers of Ilium' – inflames him with a desire that burns more brightly than 'flaming Jupiter'. But inevitably the same fire that he attempts to control is fated to destroy him. And when hell is at last revealed, the scene of conflagration is described in macabre and horrific detail (Act V, Scene II, lines 121–125):

> There are the furies, tossing damned souls
> On burning forks; their bodies boil in lead:
> There are live quarters broiling on the coals,
> That ne'er can die: this ever-burning chair
> Is for o'er-tortured souls to rest them in.

Faustus's tragedy is the tragedy of any human being who plays with fire, and it is perhaps for this reason that we experience so powerfully and so acutely both the pity and the terror of his death. For by the end of the play our dreams, like his own, are in ashes (Epilogue, lines 1–2):

> Cut is the branch that might have grown full straight,
> And burned is Apollo's laurel bough.

## The writing of Doctor Faustus

Scholars have established beyond doubt that *Doctor Faustus* was not written by Marlowe alone. Several scenes were commissioned after his death by Henslowe, the theatre manager, from two other playwrights, Samuel Rowley and William Birde – although it is by no means certain that these posthumous scenes have survived in the text as we know it. Most importantly, however, it is known that Marlowe himself worked directly with an unknown collaborator. For this reason, it is quite difficult to assess exactly how much of the play was written solely by Marlowe – although there are no doubts that he alone was responsible for all the great and serious scenes on which the reputation of *Doctor Faustus* rests.

The presence of at least one other playwright explains certain inconsistencies within the play – Mephostophilis's annoyance in Act III, Scene III, at being summoned against his will to Constantinople by 'villains' charms' is a contradiction, for instance, of his earlier claim to Faustus that he appeared of his 'own accord' rather than in response to magic. Similarly, the fact that Marlowe's collaborator was by no means as intense a poet or as skilful a craftsman as Marlowe himself accounts for the presence within the play of a notably different style of writing – both in the prose farce scenes and in the very routine and stereotyped blank verse in Act III, Scene II and the first three scenes of Act IV.

Beyond these points of interest, however, the existence of a collaborator is not an issue that need disturb a general reader of *Doctor Faustus* in any significant way. For the grand design of the play was indisputably Marlowe's own. His was the creative intelligence behind its conception. And his – alone – was the spirit and imagination that gave it shape.

## *The text of* Doctor Faustus

The earliest surviving edition of *Doctor Faustus* was printed in 1604, and reprinted – with minor alterations – in 1609 and 1611. In 1616, however, a radically different edition appeared, which was also reprinted several times. The earlier version is known as the A text; the later is described as the B text. An editor wishing to present the reader with an accurate version of the play is therefore faced with the difficult task of deciding which of the two texts should be accepted as authentic.

The principal difference between them is in length. The A

text is only 1517 lines long; the B text occupies 2121 lines. And because the main omissions in the A text are of comic scenes which Marlowe almost certainly did not write himself (the Bruno story for example and Benvolio's attempted revenge), critics originally assumed that the A text was the more reliable.

This view, however, has now been largely discredited. The additional B scenes, whether written by Marlowe or not, are described in the source book that he uses (the *Damnable Life*: see Jan Kott's personal essay, page viii) and form part of the whole design of the play. Without them, the central section is disconnected and incomplete, and the ironic contrast between Faustus's grand aspirations and trivial achievements is inadequately made. Moreover, extensive research has led to the conclusion that A is in fact an abbreviated text, probably reconstructed from memory by actors involved in productions of the play. Very possibly it was compiled specifically to meet the needs of touring companies performing the play on a bare stage, without the facilities available in a normally equipped theatre. And even though the A text contains some 200 lines not found in B, it is highly unlikely that any of these were written by Marlowe himself.

For these reasons, most modern editions of *Doctor Faustus* – including this edition – are based on the B text, in the belief that this is the text that comes closest to Marlowe's original intentions for his play.

# Doctor Faustus

# CHARACTERS
## in the play

CHORUS.

DOCTOR JOHN FAUSTUS.

WAGNER, *a student, his servant.*

VALDES,
CORNELIUS, } *friends to Faustus, magicians.*

THREE SCHOLARS, *students under Faustus.*

AN OLD MAN.

POPE ADRIAN.

RAYMOND, *King of Hungary.*

BRUNO, *the rival Pope.*

THE CARDINALS OF FRANCE AND PADUA.

THE ARCHBISHOP OF RHEIMS.

CHARLES V, *Emperor of Germany.*

MARTINO,
FREDERICK, } *gentlemen at his court.*
BENVOLIO,

THE DUKE OF SAXONY.

THE DUKE OF VANHOLT.

THE DUCHESS OF VANHOLT.

BISHOPS, MONKS, FRIARS, SOLDIERS, *and* ATTENDANTS.

ROBIN, *called the Clown.*

DICK.

A VINTNER.

A HORSE-COURSER.

A CARTER.

A HOSTESS.

GOOD ANGEL.

BAD ANGEL.

MEPHOSTOPHILIS.

LUCIFER.

BEELZEBUB.

PRIDE,
COVETOUSNESS,
ENVY,
WRATH,                    } *the Seven Deadly Sins.*
GLUTTONY,
SLOTH,
LECHERY,
ALEXANDER THE GREAT,
HIS PARAMOUR,
DARIUS, *King of Persia,*   } *spirits.*
HELEN OF TROY,
TWO CUPIDS,
DEVILS *and* A PIPER.

*The purpose of the* Prologue *is to indicate to the audience the theme of the play to come: it will be neither military, nor about love nor politics (the first six lines could possibly allude to Marlowe's earlier plays, or simply to other plays performed by the same company). Instead, it is to focus on the rise and fall of a single individual, and his place in time and space is brought skilfully into focus.*

1  Trasimene: *lake in Italy where the Romans were defeated by Hannibal in 217* BC.

2  Mars: *the Roman God of War.*
   mate: *join with; support.*
   Carthagens: *Carthaginians; citizens of the city-state of Carthage in North Africa, led by Hannibal.*

4  state: *government.*

6  muse: *poet.*
   vaunt: *display proudly.*

7  gentles: *good people.*

11  base of stock: *low in rank.*

12  Rhode: *now Stadtroda, in East Germany.*

13  Wittenberg: *city in East Germany, the seat of a famous university founded in 1502. Through Luther, (see Personal Essay, page vii) it became associated with the establishment of German Protestantism.*

14  Whereas: *where.*

16  The fruitful ... grac'd: *honoured with his presence the fruitful garden of scholarship.*

17  grac'd with doctor's name: *granted the degree of doctor. As at lines 7 and 8 ('perform/The form') Marlowe is engaging here in word play.*

20  swollen ... a self-conceit: *puffed up with a false idea of his own intellectual ability.*

21  waxen wings: *reference to the death of Icarus, recounted in Greek mythology. He flew too close to the sun which melted the wax securing his artificial wings, and he plunged into the sea.*

25  surfeits: *gorges to excess. Faustus's self-indulgence is frequently depicted through metaphors related to food and feasting.*
   necromancy: *black magic, practised by calling up the spirits of the dead.*

# Prologue

*Enter* CHORUS.

CHORUS Not marching in the fields of Trasimene
    Where Mars did mate the warlike Carthagens,
    Nor sporting in the dalliance of love
    In courts of kings where state is overturn'd,
    Nor in the pomp of proud audacious deeds
    Intends our muse to vaunt his heavenly verse:
    Only this, gentles – we must now perform
    The form of Faustus' fortunes, good or bad:
    And now to patient judgements we appeal,
    And speak for Faustus in his infancy.          10
    Now is he born, of parents base of stock,
    In Germany, within a town call'd Rhode;
    At riper years to Wittenberg he went,
    Whereas his kinsmen chiefly brought him up.
    So much he profits in divinity,
    The fruitful plot of scholarism grac'd,
    That shortly he was grac'd with doctor's name,
    Excelling all, and sweetly can dispute
    In th' heavenly matters of theology;
    Till, swollen with cunning of a self-conceit,    20
    His waxen wings did mount above his reach,
    And, melting, heavens conspir'd his overthrow;
    For, falling to a devilish exercise,
    And glutted now with learning's golden gifts,
    He surfeits upon cursed necromancy;
    Nothing so sweet as magic is to him,
    Which he prefers before his chiefest bliss:
    And this the man that in his study sits.
*Exit.*

1 Settle thy studies: *choose a specific area of study.*
2 profess: *excel in, and teach.*
3 Having ... show: *now that you have graduated, show that you are indeed a student of theology.*
4 level: *aim at; consider.*
   end: *purpose.*
5 Aristotle: *Greek philosopher (384–322 BC), author of* Prior Analytics *and* Posterior Analytics *(line 6), which consider the nature of proof in argument.*
7 Bene ... logices: (Latin) *This is translated in the following line.*

12 on kai me on: *transliteration of the Greek phrase meaning 'being and not being'.*
   Galen: *Greek physician and author of many treatises on medicine (AD 130–200).*
13 ubi desinit ... medicus: (Latin) *'where the philosopher leaves off, the doctor begins' (Aristotle).*
15 eterniz'd: *immortalized.*
16 Summum ... sanitas: (Latin) *'The greatest good of medicine is health' (Aristotle).*
19 Is not ... aphorisms?: *Do not even your casual words have the weight of medical precepts?*
20 Are not ... monuments?: *Are not your prescriptions enduring examples of medical art?*

27 Justinian: *Emperor of Constantinople who created the Roman code of law in the sixth century AD in his* Institutes *(line 32).*
28 Si una ... rei: (Latin) *'If one and the same thing is bequeathed to two people, one of them shall have the object and the other its value' (Justinian).*

# Act One

*Scene one*

<small>FAUSTUS</small> *in his study.*

<small>FAUSTUS</small> Settle thy studies, Faustus, and begin
  To sound the depth of that thou wilt profess;
  Having commenc'd, be a divine in show,
  Yet level at the end of every art,
  And live and die in Aristotle's works.
  Sweet Analytics, 'tis thou hast ravish'd me!
  *Bene disserere est finis logices.*
  Is to dispute well logic's chiefest end?
  Affords this art no greater miracle?
  Then read no more, thou hast attain'd that end;      10
  A greater subject fitteth Faustus' wit.
  Bid *on kai me on* farewell, Galen come,
  Seeing *ubi desinit philosophus, ibi incipit medicus.*
  Be a physician, Faustus, heap up gold,
  And be eterniz'd for some wondrous cure.
  *Summum bonum medicinae sanitas,*
  The end of physic is our body's health.
  Why, Faustus, hast thou not attain'd that end?
  Is not thy common talk sound aphorisms?
  Are not thy bills hung up as monuments,      20
  Whereby whole cities have escap'd the plague
  And thousand desperate maladies been cur'd?
  Yet art thou still but Faustus, and a man.
  Couldst thou make men to live eternally
  Or being dead raise them to iife again,
  Then this profession were to be esteem'd.
  Physic, farewell! Where is Justinian?
  *Si una eademque res legatur duobus, alter rem, alter valorem*
  *rei, etc.*
  A petty case of paltry legacies!      30

31 Exhereditare ... nisi –: (Latin) *'The father may not disinherit the son, except –'* *(Justinian).*

35 trash: *money (term of contempt).*

37 When all is done: *after all.*

38 Jerome's Bible: *the Vulgate, or Latin translation of the Bible, prepared mainly by Saint Jerome in AD 405.*

39 Stipendium peccati mors est: (Latin) *'The wages of sin is death',* *a quotation from* Romans VI: 23. *Notably, Faustus omits to read on: 'but the gift of God is eternal life through Jesus Christ our Lord.'*

40–1 Si peccasse ... veritas: (Latin) *Faustus quotes and then translates* I John 1: 8. *Again, he does not read on: 'If we confess our sins he is faithful and just to forgive us our sins.'*

46 Che sarà, sarà: (Italian) *The translation follows immediately.*

48 metaphysics: *supernatural sciences.*

50 Lines ... characters: *magician's stock-in-trade; devices to ward off spirits or to summon them.*

54 artisan: *craftsman.*

55 quiet poles: *the poles of the universe ('quiet' because unmoving) on which all heavenly bodies were believed to revolve.*

57 but: *only*
   several: *separate; own.*

59 his dominion ... in this: *the province of one who excels in magic.*

62 tire: *exercise strenuously; exhaust yourselves.*
   get: *beget; create.*

*Exhereditare filium non potest pater, nisi –*
Such is the subject of the Institute
And universal body of the law.
This study fits a mercenary drudge
Who aims at nothing but external trash,
Too servile and illiberal for me.
When all is done, divinity is best.
Jerome's Bible, Faustus, view it well.
*Stipendium peccati mors est.* Ha! *Stipendium, etc.* The reward
of sin is death: that's hard. *Si peccasse negamus, fallimur,*    40
*et nulla est in nobis veritas.* If we say that we have no
sin, we deceive ourselves, and there's no truth in us.
Why, then, belike we must sin, and so consequently
die.
Ay, we must die an everlasting death.
What doctrine call you this? *Che sarà, sarà*:
What will be, shall be! Divinity, adieu!
These metaphysics of magicians
And necromantic books are heavenly;
Lines, circles, letters, and characters:    50
Ay, these are those that Faustus most desires.
O, what a world of profit and delight,
Of power, of honour, of omnipotence,
Is promis'd to the studious artisan!
All things that move between the quiet poles
Shall be at my command: emperors and kings
Are but obey'd in their several provinces,
Nor can they raise the wind or rend the clouds;
But his dominion that exceeds in this
Stretcheth as far as doth the mind of man:    60
A sound magician is a demi-god;
Here tire, my brains, to get a deity!
*Enter* WAGNER.
Wagner, commend me to my dearest friends,
The German Valdes and Cornelius;
Request them earnestly to visit me.

67 conference: *conversation*.

72 that: *that book of magic*.

75 Jove: *the poetical name for Jupiter, the chief god of the Romans. Here, however, the word 'Jove' signifies God in the Christian sense.*

76 elements: *earth, water, fire and air*.

77 conceit: *the idea*.

79 Resolve ... ambiguities: *Free me from all doubts*.

80 desperate enterprise: *impossibly difficult task*.

81 India: *this could refer to either the East or the West Indies*.

82 orient: *from eastern seas*; (*more generally*) *shining*.

83 the new-found world: *probable reference to the discovery of America*.

84 delicates: *delicacies*.

87 wall...brass: *in Robert Greene's comedy* Friar Bacon and Friar Bungay *(1594), Friar Bacon (the thirteenth-century English scholar) is shown planning to wall England with brass*.

88 Rhine: *rather than the river Elbe, on which Wittenberg stands*.
   circle: *encircle*.

89 public schools: *university lecture rooms*.

90 bravely: *finely – instead of in the sober dress they were recommended to wear*.

91 levy ... coin: *buy troops with the money*.

92 Prince of Parma: *Spanish governor-general of the Netherlands from 1579 to 1592; famous soldier and England's enemy*.

94 engines: *instruments; contraptions; weapons*.
   brunt: *assault; violent attack*.

95 fiery keel: *fire ship – that is a ship carrying combustibles set adrift among enemy ships. In 1585, during the siege of Antwerp, such a ship was used by the Dutch to destroy the bridge built by the Prince of Parma over the River Scheldt*.

WAGNER  I will, sir.

*Exit.*

FAUSTUS  Their conference will be a greater help to me
    Than all my labours, plod I ne'er so fast.

*Enter the* ANGEL *and* SPIRIT.

GOOD ANGEL  O Faustus, lay that damned book aside
    And gaze not on it lest it tempt thy soul       70
    And heap God's heavy wrath upon thy head.
    Read, read the scriptures; that is blasphemy.

BAD ANGEL  Go forward, Faustus, in that famous art
    Wherein all nature's treasury is contain'd:
    Be thou on earth as Jove as in the sky,
    Lord and commander of these elements.

*Exeunt* ANGELS.

FAUSTUS  How am I glutted with conceit of this!
    Shall I make spirits fetch me what I please,
    Resolve me of all ambiguities,
    Perform what desperate enterprise I will?     80
    I'll have them fly to India for gold,
    Ransack the ocean for orient pearl,
    And search all corners of the new-found world
    For pleasant fruits and princely delicates;
    I'll have them read me strange philosophy
    And tell the secrets of all foreign kings;
    I'll have them wall all Germany with brass
    And make swift Rhine circle fair Wittenberg;
    I'll have them fill the public schools with silk
    Wherewith the students shall be bravely clad;     90
    I'll levy soldiers with the coin they bring
    And chase the Prince of Parma from our land
    And reign sole king of all our provinces;
    Yea, stranger engines for the brunt of war
    Than was the fiery keel at Antwerp's bridge
    I'll make my servile spirits to invent.

*Enter* VALDES *and* CORNELIUS.
    Come, German Valdes and Cornelius,

98 sage: *wise*.

101 concealed: *occult*.
102 fantasy: *imagination*.
103 receive no object: *accept no objections*.
104 But: *only*.

106 wits: *minds*.
107 basest of the three: *even lower than the other three*.

111 syllogisms: *logical arguments*.
112 Gravell'd: *defeated; puzzled*.
113 flowering pride: *best students*.
114 problems: *topics of scholarly debate*.
115 Musaeus: *legendary pre-Homeric Greek poet, said to be a pupil of Orpheus. Virgil's* Aeneid *includes a glimpse of Musaeus in the Underworld (VI; 666–7), and* Georgics IV *tells of spirits swarming round Orpheus himself*.
116 Agrippa: *Henry Cornelius Agrippa von Nettesheim (1486–1535), humanist and reputed magician, famous for invoking spirits ('shadows') of the dead*.
118 wit: *intelligence*.
119 canonize: *enter our names in the records of famous people*.
120 Indian Moors: *American Indians. Spain had conquered parts of South America*.
124 Almain...staves: *German cavalrymen with lances*.
127 Shadowing: *harbouring*.
    airy: *heavenly*.
128 queen of love: *the Goddess Venus*.
129 argosies: *treasure ships*.
130 golden fleece: *reference to Greek mythology and the journey of Jason and the Argonauts in search of the golden fleece. In a similar way, Valdes remarks, the gold of America is borne back annually by the Spanish to the treasury of King Philip II (1527–98) of Spain*.

And make me blest with your sage conference.
Valdes, sweet Valdes, and Cornelius,
Know that your words have won me at the last          100
To practise magic and concealed arts;
Yet not your words only, but mine own fantasy,
That will receive no object, for my head
But ruminates on necromantic skill.
Philosophy is odious and obscure,
Both law and physic are for petty wits,
Divinity is basest of the three,
Unpleasant, harsh, contemptible, and vile;
'Tis magic, magic, that hath ravish'd me.
Then, gentle friends, aid me in this attempt,          110
And I, that have with concise syllogisms
Gravell'd the pastors of the German church,
And made the flowering pride of Wittenberg
Swarm to my problems as the infernal spirits
On sweet Musaeus when he came to hell,
Will be as cunning as Agrippa was,
Whose shadows made all Europe honour him.
VALDES Faustus, these books, thy wit, and our experience
Shall make all nations to canonize us.
As Indian Moors obey their Spanish lords,          120
So shall the spirits of every element
Be always serviceable to us three:
Like lions shall they guard us when we please,
Like Almain rutters with their horsemen's staves
Or Lapland giants trotting by our sides;
Sometimes like women or unwedded maids,
Shadowing more beauty in their airy brows
Than in the white breasts of the queen of love.
From Venice shall they drag huge argosies,
And from America the golden fleece          130
That yearly stuffs old Philip's treasury,
If learned Faustus will be resolute.
FAUSTUS Valdes, as resolute am I in this

134 object it not: *do not make it an objection.*

137 grounded in: *well schooled in.*

138 Enrich'd with tongues: *skilled in languages. Greek, Hebrew and – especially – Latin were the languages considered necessary to communicate with spirits.*
well seen in minerals: *with extensive knowledge of the properties of minerals.*

139 principles: *rudiments; basics.*

141 frequented for this mystery: *sought after for practising this art.*

142 Delphian oracle: *the oracle of Apollo at Delphi, on the slope of Mount Parnassus, where divine advice could be obtained in ancient Greece.*

146 massy: *huge.*

150 conjure: *call up spirits.*
lusty: *pleasant.*

153 Bacon: *Roger Bacon (1214–92). See note to line 87.*
Abanus: *Pietro d'Abano (c. 1250–1316), Italian physician and philosopher who was also reputed to be a magician.*

154 The Hebrew Psalter, and New Testament: *the Psalms in the Old Testament and the opening verses of the Gospel of St John in the New Testament were often used in conjuring spirits.*

157 words of art: *magic words (to summon spirits).*

163 canvass every quiddity: *discuss every detail.*

165 therefor: *because of it.*

14

As thou to live; therefore object it not.

CORNELIUS The miracles that magic will perform
    Will make thee vow to study nothing else.
    He that is grounded in astrology,
    Enrich'd with tongues, well seen in minerals,
    Hath all the principles magic doth require;
    Then doubt not, Faustus, but to be renown'd    140
    And more frequented for this mystery
    Than heretofore the Delphian oracle.
    The spirits tell me they can dry the sea
    And fetch the treasure of all foreign wrecks,
    Ay, all the wealth that our forefathers hid
    Within the massy entrails of the earth.
    Then tell me, Faustus, what shall we three want?

FAUSTUS Nothing, Cornelius. O, this cheers my soul!
    Come, show me some demonstrations magical,
    That I may conjure in some lusty grove    150
    And have these joys in full possession.

VALDES Then haste thee to some solitary grove,
    And bear wise Bacon's and Abanus' works,
    The Hebrew Psalter, and New Testament;
    And whatsoever else is requisite
    We will inform thee ere our conference cease.

CORNELIUS Valdes, first let him know the words of art,
    And then, all other ceremonies learn'd,
    Faustus may try his cunning by himself.

VALDES First I'll instruct thee in the rudiments,    160
    And then wilt thou be perfecter than I.

FAUSTUS Then come and dine with me, and after meat
    We'll canvass every quiddity thereof,
    For ere I sleep I'll try what I can do:
    This night I'll conjure though I die therefor.

*Exeunt omnes.*

2 sic probo: (Latin) *'Thus I prove it'; term used in scholastic argument.*

3 presently: *at once.*

4 boy: *servant.*

8 that follows not: *that is not a logical consequence. Wagner is parodying the techniques of intellectual debate.*

9 Go to: *come along!*

12 licentiates: *graduates, able to proceed to a Master's or Doctor's degree.*

stand: *rely.*

16 dunces: *idiots.*

17 corpus naturale: (Latin) *'natural body'.*

mobile: (Latin) *'capable of movement'. Wagner is quoting from Aristotle.*

21 place of execution: *here, the dining room.*

24 precisian: *Puritan. The solemn manner of Puritans was often mocked in contemporary drama.*

26 this wine: *carried by Wagner.*

## Scene two

*Enter two* SCHOLARS.

1 SCHOLAR I wonder what's become of Faustus, that was
wont to make our schools ring with *sic probo*.

*Enter* WAGNER.

2 SCHOLAR That shall we presently know; here comes his
boy.

1 SCHOLAR How now, sirrah, where's thy master?

WAGNER God in heaven knows.

2 SCHOLAR Why, dost not thou know then?

WAGNER Yes, I know; but that follows not.

1 SCHOLAR Go to, sirrah, leave your jesting and tell us
where he is.                                                        10

WAGNER That follows not by force of argument, which
you, being licentiates, should stand upon; therefore ack-
nowledge your error and be attentive.

2 SCHOLAR Then you will not tell us?

WAGNER You are deceived, for I will tell you. Yet, if you
were not dunces, you would never ask me such a question. For is he not *corpus naturale*? and is not that *mobile*?
Then wherefore should you ask me such a question? But
that I am by nature phlegmatic, slow to wrath, and pro-
ne to lechery (to love, I would say), it were not for you      20
to come within forty foot of the place of execution –
although I do not doubt but to see you both hanged the
next sessions. Thus having triumphed over you, I will
set my countenance like a precisian and begin to speak
thus: Truly, my dear brethren, my master is within at
dinner with Valdes and Cornelius, as this wine, if it
could speak, would inform your worships: and so the
Lord bless you, preserve you, and keep you, my dear
brethren.

*Exit.*

1 SCHOLAR O Faustus, then I fear that which I have long      30
suspected,

34 not ally'd to me: *not a friend and associate.*

36 Rector: *head of the university.*

2 Orion's drizzling look: *the star constellahon Orion ('the hunter') was traditionally associated with rain. See* Aeneid I: 535 *and* IV: 52.

3 th'antarctic world: *Marlowe apparently believed that night advanced from the south (rather than the west).*

4 welkin: *sky.*

6 hest: *command.*

7 pray'd and sacrific'd: *necessary preliminary to conjuring.*

8 this circle: *traditionally, a magician protected himself by drawing a circle on the ground. So long as it remained unbroken and he stayed within it, no evil spirit could harm him.*

9 anagrammatiz'd: *the letters re-arranged to form new words.*

10 breviated: *shortened.*

11 adjunct to: *heavenly body fixed to, or suspended in, the sky.*

12 characters of signs and erring stars: *symbols of the signs of the Zodiac and the planets.*

16–19 Sint Mihi ... Mephostophilis: (Latin) *'May the gods of the underworld be favourable to me! Away with the threefold spirit of Jehovah [God's Holy Trinity]! Hail, spirits of fire, air, water and earth! Lucifer, prince of the east, Beelzebub, monarch of burning hell, and Demogorgon: we ask your favour that Mephostophilis may appear and rise!'*

That thou art fallen into that damned art
For which they two are infamous through the world.
2 SCHOLAR Were he a stranger, not ally'd to me,
The danger of his soul would make me mourn.
But come, let us go and inform the Rector:
It may be his grave counsel may reclaim him.
1 SCHOLAR I fear me, nothing will reclaim him now.
2 SCHOLAR Yet let us see what we can do.
*Exeunt.*

## Scene three

*Thunder. Enter* LUCIFER *and four* DEVILS [*above*]:
FAUSTUS *to them with this speech.*
FAUSTUS Now that the gloomy shadow of the night,
Longing to view Orion's drizzling look,
Leaps from th' antarctic world unto the sky
And dims the welkin with her pitchy breath,
Faustus, begin thine incantations,
And try if devils will obey thy hest,
Seeing thou hast pray'd and sacrific'd to them.
Within this circle is Jehovah's name
Forward and backward anagrammatiz'd,
The breviated names of holy saints,                          10
Figures of every adjunct to the heavens,
And characters of signs and erring stars,
By which the spirits are enforc'd to rise:
Then fear not, Faustus, to be resolute
And try the uttermost magic can perform.
*Thunder.*
*Sint mihi dei Acherontis propitii! Valeat numen triplex Iehovae!*
*Ignei, aerii, aquatici, terreni spiritus salvete! Orientis princeps*
*Lucifer, Beelzebub inferni ardentis monarcha, et Demogorgon,*
*propitiamus vos ut appareat et surgat Mephostophilis!*

[Dragon *appears briefly above*].

20–22 Quid tu ... Mephostophilis!: (Latin) *Why do you delay?*
*By Jehovah, Gehenna* [hell]*, and the holy water which I now sprink-*
*le, and by the sign of the cross which I now make, and by our prayers,*
*let Mephostophilis himself now rise, compelled to serve us.*

27 virtue: *power.*

32 conjuror laureate: *magician worthy of special distinction.*
34 Quin ... imagine!: (Latin) *'Why do you not return, Mephos-*
*tophilis, in the likeness of a friar?'*

36 charge: *order.*

39 overwhelm: *flood.*

46 per accidens: (Latin) *as it appeared. In other words, the spells*
*summoned Mephostophilis not because of what they themselves were,*
*but because of what they represented and happened to include.*
47 rack: *violate.*
48 Abjure: *renounce.*

*Quid tu moraris? Per Iehovam, Gehennam, et consecratam*  20
*aquam quam nunc spargo, signumque crucis quod nunc facio, et*
*per vota nostra, ipse nunc surgat nobis dicatus Mephostophilis!*

*Enter a* DEVIL.

    I charge thee to return and change thy shape;
    Thou art too ugly to attend on me.
    Go, and return an old Franciscan friar,
    That holy shape becomes a devil best.

*Exit* Devil.

    I see there's virtue in my heavenly words.
    Who would not be proficient in this art?
    How pliant is this Mephostophilis,
    Full of obedience and humility!  30
    Such is the force of magic and my spells.
    Now, Faustus, thou art conjuror laureate,
    That canst command great Mephostophilis.
    *Quin redis, Mephostophilis, fratris imagine!*

*Enter* MEPHOSTOPHILIS.

MEPHOSTOPHILIS  Now, Faustus, what wouldst thou have
    me do?

FAUSTUS  I charge thee wait upon me whilst I live,
    To do whatever Faustus shall command,
    Be it to make the moon drop from her sphere
    Or the ocean to overwhelm the world.

MEPHOSTOPHILIS  I am a servant to great Lucifer  40
    And may not follow thee without his leave;
    No more than he commands must we perform.

FAUSTUS  Did not he charge thee to appear to me?

MEPHOSTOPHILIS  No, I came hither of mine own accord.

FAUSTUS  Did not my conjuring speeches raise thee? Speak.

MEPHOSTOPHILIS  That was the cause, but yet *per accidens*:
    For when we hear one rack the name of God,
    Abjure the scriptures and his saviour Christ,
    We fly, in hope to get his glorious soul;
    Nor will we come unless he use such means  50
    Whereby he is in danger to be damn'd.

55–56 So Faustus ... already done: *see note to line 16.*

60 he confounds hell in Elysium: *he does not distinguish between the Christian concept of hell and the Greek concept of an after-life in Elysium.*

61 His ghost ... philosophers!: *his spirit is with those Greek philosophers (who shared his disbelief in eternal punishment).*

68 by aspiring pride: *Lucifer's pride led him to aim too high. Note the recurrent images of ascent, flight and fall which echo the pattern of the play.*

76 Why, this is hell, nor am I out of it: *compare this realization with the words of Satan in Milton's* Paradise Lost *IV: 75: 'Which way I fly is Hell; myself am Hell.'*

81 demands: *questions.*

83 passionate: *moved by powerful feeling.*

Therefore the shortest cut for conjuring
Is stoutly to abjure the Trinity
And pray devoutly to the prince of hell.
FAUSTUS So Faustus hath
Already done, and holds this principle,
There is no chief but only Beelzebub,
To whom Faustus doth dedicate himself.
This word 'damnation' terrifies not him,
For he confounds hell in Elysium:                                    60
His ghost be with the old philosophers!
But, leaving these vain trifles of men's souls,
Tell me, what is that Lucifer thy lord?
MEPHOSTOPHILIS Arch-regent and commander of all spir-
    its.
FAUSTUS Was not that Lucifer an angel once?
MEPHOSTOPHILIS Yes, Faustus, and most dearly lov'd of
    God.
FAUSTUS How comes it then that he is prince of devils?
MEPHOSTOPHILIS O, by aspiring pride and insolence,
For which God threw him from the face of heaven.
FAUSTUS And what are you that live with Lucifer?           70
MEPHOSTOPHILIS Unhappy spirits that fell with Lucifer,
Conspir'd against our God with Lucifer,
And are for ever damn'd with Lucifer.
FAUSTUS Where are you damn'd?
MEPHOSTOPHILIS                                  In hell.
FAUSTUS How comes it then that thou art out of hell?
MEPHOSTOPHILIS Why, this is hell, nor am I out of it.
Think'st thou that I, who saw the face of God
And tasted the eternal joys of heaven,
Am not tormented with ten thousand hells
In being depriv'd of everlasting bliss?                              80
O Faustus, leave these frivolous demands,
Which strike a terror to my fainting soul.
FAUSTUS What, is great Mephostophilis so passionate
For being deprived of the joys of heaven?

85 manly: *note the strength of Faustus's belief in human potential –
and also the irony that he should recommend manliness to a supernatural being.*

89 Jove's deity: *the divinity of God. As in Scene I, line 75, the name
'Jove' is used to signify the Christian God.*

91 So: *on condition that.*

100 resolve: *inform.*
mind: *decision.*

105 thorough: *through.*
106 pass: *cross over.*
107 bind: *enclose. Faustus is referring to the hills on either side of the
straits of Gilbraltar. If they were joined, Africa would be united
with Spain, and hence with Europe.*
108 continent to: *continuous with; joined by land.*
109 contributory: *subject.*
110 leave: *permission.*
113 speculation: *intense study.*

Learn thou of Faustus manly fortitude
And scorn those joys thou never shalt possess.
Go bear these tidings to great Lucifer:
Seeing Faustus hath incurr'd eternal death
By desperate thoughts against Jove's deity,
Say he surrenders up to him his soul                              90
So he will spare him four-and-twenty years,
Letting him live in all voluptuousness,
Having thee ever to attend on me,
To give me whatsoever I shall ask,
To tell me whatsoever I demand,
To slay mine enemies and aid my friends,
And always be obedient to my will.
Go, and return to mighty Lucifer,
And meet me in my study at midnight,
And then resolve me of thy master's mind.                         100
MEPHOSTOPHILIS  I will, Faustus.
*Exit.*

FAUSTUS  Had I as many souls as there be stars,
I'd give them all for Mephostophilis.
By him I'll be great emperor of the world,
And make a bridge thorough the moving air
To pass the ocean with a band of men;
I'll join the hills that bind the Afric shore
And make that country continent to Spain,
And both contributory to my crown;
The Emperor shall not live but by my leave,                       110
Nor any potentate of Germany.
Now that I have obtain'd what I desire,
I'll live in speculation of this art
Till Mephostophilis return again.
*Exit.*
[*Exeunt* LUCIFER *and* Devils.]

2 Zounds: *By God's wounds! (an oath)*.

3 pickedevants: *beards fashionably cut to a small point.*

5 comings in: *income; earnings.*

6 goings out: *expenses. Robin is using the phrase in two ways, however, for he points to the tattered clothes through which parts of his body are protruding.*

8 villain: *wretch.*

out of service: *without a job.*

9 give his soul to the devil: *note how this scene is parodying the main action of the play.*

14 Qui mihi discipulus: (Latin) *'You who are my pupil'. These are the opening words of 'Carmen de moribus', a poem much read in Elizabethan grammar schools and written by William Lily (1466? – 1522).*

16 beaten: *embroidered. Wagner is punning here, for his promise to dress his servant in silk also suggests that he will thrash him.*

stavesacre: *flea powder; seeds that destroy vermin.*

17 belike: *probably.*

20 presently: *immediately.*

22 familiars: *devils attendant on a human being.*

23–4 they are as familiar . . . drink: *they treat me with as little ceremony as if they were customers at an inn who pay for what they consume (i.e. my flesh and blood). Robin is using the word 'familiar' in a different sense here.*

27 guilders: *Dutch coins; here, hiring money.*

29 warning: *notice.*

31 again: *back.*

32 pressed: *hired; enlisted.*

## Scene four

*Enter* WAGNER *and the* Clown [ROBIN].

WAGNER  Come hither, sirrah boy.

ROBIN  Boy! O, disgrace to my person! Zounds, boy in
your face! You have seen many boys with such pickedevants, I am sure.

WAGNER  Sirrah, hast thou no comings in?

ROBIN  Yes, and goings out too, you may see, sir.

WAGNER  Alas, poor slave! see how poverty jests in his
nakedness. I know the villain's out of service, and so
hungry that I know he would give his soul to the devil
for a shoulder of mutton, though it were blood-raw.      10

ROBIN  Not so, neither. I had need to have it well roasted,
and good sauce to it, if I pay so dear, I can tell you.

WAGNER  Sirrah, wilt thou be my man and wait on me?
and I will make thee go like *Qui mihi discipulus.*

ROBIN  What, in verse?

WAGNER  No, slave, in beaten silk and stavesacre.

ROBIN  Stavesacre! that's good to kill vermin. Then, belike,
if I serve you, I shall be lousy.

WAGNER  Why, so thou shalt be, whether thou dost it or
no; for, sirrah, if thou dost not presently bind thyself to     20
me for seven years, I'll turn all the lice about thee into
familiars and make them tear thee in pieces.

ROBIN  Nay, sir, you may save yourself a labour, for they
are as familiar with me as if they paid for their meat and
drink, I can tell you.

WAGNER  Well, sirrah, leave your jesting and take these
guilders.

ROBIN  Yes, marry, sir, and I thank you too.

WAGNER  So, now thou art to be at an hour's warning,
whensoever and wheresoever the devil shall fetch thee.     30

ROBIN  Here, take your guilders again, I'll none of 'em.

WAGNER  Not I, thou art pressed, prepare thyself, for I will

33–34 Banio! Belcher!: *invented by Wagner. The former is possibly a corruption of Belial.*

35 And: *If.*

belch: *eject violently. Robin is punning on the name 'Belcher'.*

45 brave: *fine; wonderful.*

49 diametrally: *diametrically; in a straight line.*

50 quasi . . . insistere: (Latin) *tread, as it were, in our footsteps.*

presently raise up two devils to carry thee away. Banio!
Belcher!

ROBIN Belcher! And Belcher come here, I'll belch him. I
am not afraid of a devil.

*Enter two* Devils, *and the* Clown *runs up and down crying*.

WAGNER How now, sir, will you serve me now?

ROBIN Ay, good Wagner, take away the devil then.

WAGNER Spirits, away!

*Exeunt* [Devils].

Now, sirrah, follow me.                                    40

ROBIN I will, sir. But hark you, master, will you teach me
this conjuring occupation?

WAGNER Ay, sirrah, I'll teach thee to turn thyself to a dog,
or a cat, or a mouse, or a rat, or anything.

ROBIN A dog, or a cat, or a mouse, or a rat! O brave, Wagner!

WAGNER Villain, call me Master Wagner, and see that
you walk attentively, and let your right eye be always
diametrally fixed upon my left heel, that thou mayest
*quasi vestigiis nostris insistere*.                       50

ROBIN Well, sir, I warrant you.

*Exeunt*.

3 What boots it?: *What does it avail? What could be the point?*

6 be resolute: *firm resolve was advocated by Valdes in Act I, Scene I, line 132. Faustus's striving here (and in Act I, Scene III, line 14) to be 'resolute' indicates his irrational conviction that stubbornness is a heroic quality.*

11 appetite: *desire. Note the effectiveness of constant references to excessive and illicit feasting, which recall (among other things) the story of the forbidden fruit growing on the Tree of Knowledge in the Garden of Eden, which tempted Adam and Eve.*

15 Go forward . . . famous art: *repetition of Act I, Scene I, line 73.*

17 what of these?: *what use are these?*

24 signory: *lordship; governorship.*
   Emden: *wealthy port on the mouth of the river Ems, in north-west Germany. At the time, it traded extensively with England.*

# Act Two

*Scene one*

*Enter* FAUSTUS *in his study.*

FAUSTUS  Now, Faustus, must thou needs be damn'd
    And canst thou not be sav'd?
    What boots it then to think of God or heaven?
    Away with such vain fancies, and despair;
    Despair in God, and trust in Beelzebub.
    Now go not backward; no, Faustus, be resolute:
    Why waver'st thou? O, something soundeth in mine
      ears,
    'Abjure this magic, turn to God again!'
    Ay, and Faustus will turn to God again.
    To God? He loves thee not;                10
    The god thou serv'st is thine own appetite,
    Wherein is fix'd the love of Beelzebub:
    To him I'll build an altar and a church
    And offer lukewarm blood of new-born babes.

*Enter the two* Angels.

BAD ANGEL  Go forward, Faustus, in that famous art.

GOOD ANGEL  Sweet Faustus, leave that execrable art.

FAUSTUS  Contrition, prayer, repentance, what of these?

GOOD ANGEL  O, they are means to bring thee unto heaven.

BAD ANGEL  Rather illusions, fruits of lunacy,
    That make men foolish that do use them most.      20

GOOD ANGEL  Sweet Faustus, think of heaven and heavenly
    things.

BAD ANGEL  No, Faustus, think of honour and of wealth.

*Exeunt* Angels.

FAUSTUS  Wealth!
    Why, the signory of Emden shall be mine.
    When Mephostophilis shall stand by me,
    What power can hurt me? Faustus, thou art safe:

27 Cast: *consider*.

30 Veni, veni, Mephostophilis!: (Latin) '*Come, O come, Mephos-tophilis!*'

33 So: *on condition that*.
34 hazarded: *risked*.

36 that security craves Lucifer: *note the irony that Faustus is now accepting something that is very similar to the legalities that he dismissed previously as 'too servile and illiberal' (Act I, Scene I, line 36).*

42 Solamen ... doloris: (Latin) '*It is a comfort to the miserable to have companions in their misery.*' *The source of this quotation is unknown.*

43 other: *others*.

47 wit: *mental capacity*.
48 him: *to Lucifer (since Mephostophilis is merely 'a servant to Great Lucifer' – see Act I, Scene III, line 40).*

50 bind: *give a bond for*.

54 proper: *own*.
55 Assures: *conveys by deed*.
56 regent: *ruling prince*.

Cast no more doubts! Mephostophilis, come,
And bring glad tidings from great Lucifer.
Is't not midnight? Come, Mephostophilis,
*Veni, veni, Mephostophilis!*                                     30
*Enter* MEPHOSTOPHILIS.
   Now tell me what saith Lucifer thy lord?
MEPHOSTOPHILIS That I shall wait on Faustus whilst he
      lives,
   So he will buy my service with his soul.
FAUSTUS Already Faustus hath hazarded that for thee.
MEPHOSTOPHILIS But now thou must bequeath it
      solemnly
   And write a deed of gift with thine own blood,
   For that security craves Lucifer.
   If thou deny it, I must back to hell.
FAUSTUS Stay, Mephostophilis, and tell me what good
   Will my soul do thy lord?
MEPHOSTOPHILIS                    Enlarge his kingdom.    40
FAUSTUS Is that the reason why he tempts us thus?
MEPHOSTOPHILIS *Solamen miseris socios habuisse doloris.*
FAUSTUS Why, have you any pain that torture other?
MEPHOSTOPHILIS As great as have the human souls of men.
   But tell me, Faustus, shall I have thy soul?
   And I will be thy slave and wait on thee
   And give thee more than thou hast wit to ask.
FAUSTUS Ay, Mephostophilis, I'll give it him.
MEPHOSTOPHILIS Then, Faustus, stab thy arm courageous-
      ly,
   And bind thy soul, that at some certain day          50
   Great Lucifer may claim it as his own;
   And then be thou as great as Lucifer.
FAUSTUS Lo, Mephostophilis, for love of thee
   Faustus hath cut his arm, and with his proper blood
   Assures his soul to be great Lucifer's,
   Chief lord and regent of perpetual night.
   View here this blood that trickles from mine arm,

58 propitious: *favourable; auspicious*.

63 fire to dissolve it: *no earthly fire, of course, could liquefy congealed blood*.
  straight: *immediately*.

64 staying: *standing still*.
  portend: *foretell; be an omen of*.

s.d. chafer: *portable grate*.

70 set it on: *put the saucer of blood on the chafer*.

74 Consummatum est: (Latin) *'It is finished.'* These were the last words of Jesus Christ on the cross (see John XIX: 30), and Faustus's use of them is therefore shockingly blasphemous.

77 Homo fuge!: (Latin) *'Fly, O man!'*

83 show: *pageant; procession*.

And let it be propitious for my wish.

MEPHOSTOPHILIS But, Faustus,
  Write it in manner of a deed of gift. 60

FAUSTUS Ay, so I do. But, Mephostophilis,
  My blood congeals, and I can write no more.

MEPHOSTOPHILIS I'll fetch thee fire to dissolve it straight.
*Exit.*

FAUSTUS What might the staying of my blood portend?
  Is it unwilling I should write this bill?
  Why streams it not, that I may write afresh?
  'Faustus gives to thee his soul': O, there it stay'd.
  Why shouldst thou not? is not thy soul thine own?
  Then write again: 'Faustus gives to thee his soul'.

*Enter* MEPHOSTOPHILIS *with the chafer of fire.*

MEPHOSTOPHILIS See, Faustus, here is fire; set it on. 70

FAUSTUS So, now the blood begins to clear again:
  Now will I make an end immediately.

MEPHOSTOPHILIS [*Aside*] What will not I do to obtain his
    soul!

FAUSTUS *Consummatum est*: this bill is ended,
  And Faustus hath bequeath'd his soul to Lucifer.
  But what is this inscription on mine arm?
  *Homo fuge!* Whither should I fly?
  If unto God, he'll throw me down to hell. –
  My senses are deceiv'd, here's nothing writ. –
  O yes, I see it plain; even here is writ, 80
  *Homo fuge!* Yet shall not Faustus fly.

MEPHOSTOPHILIS [*Aside*] I'll fetch him somewhat to de-
    light his mind.
*Exit.*

*Enter* Devils, *giving crowns and rich apparel to* FAUSTUS. *They dance
and then depart.*

*Enter* MEPHOSTOPHILIS.

FAUSTUS What means this show? Speak, Mephostophilis.

MEPHOSTOPHILIS Nothing, Faustus, but to delight thy
    mind

35

90 conditionally: *on condition*.
91 covenants and articles: *agreements and stipulations*.

93 effect: *carry out*.

95–109 On these ... wheresoever: *much of the legal terminology in this document is still current*.

100 whatsoever: *that is, whatever he wants*.

104 these presents: *these legal articles; this document*.

107–108 the articles above written inviolate: *the above conditions having not been broken*.
109 habitation wheresoever: *dwelling-place, wherever it is*.

112 on't: *of it*.

114 question with thee: *ask you questions*.

118 these elements: *the four elements of earth, water, fire and air*.

And let thee see what magic can perform.

FAUSTUS  But may I raise such spirits when I please?

MEPHOSTOPHILIS  Ay, Faustus, and do greater things than
  these.

FAUSTUS  Then, Mephostophilis, receive this scroll,
  A deed of gift of body and of soul:
  But yet conditionally that thou perform                                    90
  All covenants and articles between us both.

MEPHOSTOPHILIS  Faustus, I swear by hell and Lucifer
  To effect all promises between us made.

FAUSTUS  Then hear me read it, Mephostophilis.
  *On these conditions following:*
    *First, that Faustus may be a spirit in form and substance;*
  *Secondly, that Mephostophilis shall be his servant and at his*
  *command;*
    *Thirdly, that Mephostophilis shall do for him and bring him*
  *whatsoever;*                                                              100
    *Fourthly, that he shall be in his chamber or house invisible;*
    *Lastly, that he shall appear to the said John Faustus at all*
  *times in what form or shape soever he please;*
    *I, John Faustus of Wittenberg, doctor, by these presents do*
  *give both body and soul to Lucifer, prince of the east, and his*
  *minister Mephostophilis, and furthermore grant unto them that,*
  *four-and-twenty years being expired, the articles above written*
  *inviolate, full power to fetch or carry the said John Faustus, body*
  *and soul, flesh, blood, or goods, into their habitation wheresoever.*
                                              *By me John Faustus.*        110

MEPHOSTOPHILIS  Speak, Faustus, do you deliver this as
  your deed?

FAUSTUS  Ay, take it, and the devil give thee good on't!

MEPHOSTOPHILIS  Now, Faustus, ask what thou wilt.

FAUSTUS  First will I question with thee about hell.
  Tell me, where is the place that men call hell?

MEPHOSTOPHILIS  Under the heavens.

FAUSTUS  Ay, so are all things else; but whereabouts?

MEPHOSTOPHILIS  Within the bowels of these elements,

120 circumscrib'd: *bounded; confined.*
121 one self place: *one particular place.*

123 when all the world dissolves: *that is, at Doomsday, when the whole world is destroyed by fire.*
125 is: *this verb is governed by 'All places'; the phrase is singular in concept, being equivalent to 'everywhere'. Singular and plural verb forms were more flexible in Marlowe's time, as can also be noted in Shakespeare's plays.*

132 fond: *foolish.*

135 instance: *example.*

137 and: *if.*

142–143 talk not of a wife: *marriage is a holy sacrament, so such talk is heretical within the kingdom of Lucifer.*

Where we are tortur'd and remain for ever.
Hell hath no limits, nor is circumscrib'd                      120
In one self place, but where we are is hell,
And where hell is, there must we ever be;
And, to be short, when all the world dissolves
And every creature shall be purify'd,
All places shall be hell that is not heaven.

FAUSTUS I think hell's a fable.

MEPHOSTOPHILIS Ay, think so still, till experience change
  thy mind.

FAUSTUS Why, dost thou think that Faustus shall be
  damn'd?

MEPHOSTOPHILIS Ay, of necessity, for here's the scroll
  In which thou hast given thy soul to Lucifer.              130

FAUSTUS Ay, and body too; but what of that?
Think'st thou that Faustus is so fond to imagine
That after this life there is any pain?
No, these are trifles and mere old wives' tales.

MEPHOSTOPHILIS But I am an instance to prove the contrary,
For I tell thee I am damn'd and now in hell.

FAUSTUS Nay, and this be hell, I'll willingly be damn'd:
What, sleeping, eating, walking, and disputing!
But, leaving this, let me have a wife, the fairest maid in
Germany, for I am wanton and lascivious and cannot    140
live without a wife.

MEPHOSTOPHILIS How, a wife! I prithee, Faustus, talk not
  of a wife.

FAUSTUS Nay, sweet Mephostophilis, fetch me one, for I
  will have one.

MEPHOSTOPHILIS Well, thou wilt have one. Sit there till I
  come; I'll fetch thee a wife in the devil's name.
[*Exit.*]
*Enter with a* Devil *dressed like a woman, with fireworks*.
Tell me, Faustus, how dost thou like thy wife?

FAUSTUS Here's a hot whore indeed! No, I'll no wife.

150 but: *only.*

    a ceremonial toy: *trifling ritual.*

152 cull: *pick.*

    courtesans: *high-class prostitutes.*

155 Penelope: *the faithful wife of Ulysses, whose story is told in Homer's epic poem, the* Odyssey. *She resisted all suitors during her husband's absence of twenty years.*

156 Saba: *the Queen of Sheba, who visited Solomon with 'hard questions'* (1 Kings, X).

158 peruse: *read through; study.*

159 iterating: *repeating.*

160 framing: *forming.*

163 harness: *armour.*

165 fain: *gladly.*

s.d. There turn to them: *Mephostophilis indicates to Faustus that the instructions he seeks can be found in the book already given to him.*

170 characters: *symbols.*

171 dispositions: *situations (an astrological term).*

178 warrant: *assure; promise.*

MEPHOSTOPHILIS  Marriage is but a ceremonial toy;                    150
    And if thou lov'st me, think no more of it.
    I'll cull thee out the fairest courtesans
    And bring them every morning to thy bed;
    She whom thine eye shall like, thy heart shall have,
    Were she as chaste as was Penelope,
    As wise as Saba, or as beautiful
    As was bright Lucifer before his fall.
    Hold; take this book, peruse it thoroughly:
    The iterating of these lines brings gold;
    The framing of this circle on the ground                    160
    Brings thunder, whirlwinds, storm, and lightning;
    Pronounce this thrice devoutly to thyself
    And men in harness shall appear to thee,
    Ready to execute what thou command'st.

FAUSTUS  Thanks, Mephostophilis; yet fain would I have a
    book wherein I might behold all spells and incantations,
    that I might raise up spirits when I please.

MEPHOSTOPHILIS  Here they are in this book.

*There turn to them.*

FAUSTUS  Now would I have a book where I might see all
    characters of planets of the heavens, that I might know    170
    their motions and dispositions.

MEPHOSTOPHILIS  Here they are, too.

*Turn to them.*

FAUSTUS  Nay, let me have one book more, and then I have
    done, wherein I might see all plants, herbs, and trees
    that grow upon the earth.

MEPHOSTOPHILIS  Here they be.

FAUSTUS  O, thou art deceived.

MEPHOSTOPHILIS  Tut, I warrant thee.

*Turn to them. Exeunt.*

[*Here a scene is probably lost. It may well have shown the Clown, Robin,
    after stealing one of Faustus' books of magic, leaving Wagner's service
    to become an ostler at an inn.*]

7 thou or any man that breathes on earth: *Mephostophilis is here echoing Faustus's own humanist belief in 'manly' values, already voiced in Act I, Scene III, line 85 and in Act II, Scene I, line 69.*

12 yet: *still; even now.*

13 spirit: *devil.*

14 buzzeth: *whispers.*

15 Be I a devil: *even if I am a devil.*

20 thunders: *plural verb, governed by 'echoes'.*

22 halters: *hangman's ropes.*

23 dispatch: *kill.*

26 blind Homer: *the Greek epic poet, author of the* Iliad *and the* Odyssey, *was reputed to be blind.*

27 Alexander: *Homer's name for Paris, son of King Priam of Troy. The* Iliad *describes his desertion of Oenone for Helen – whom he brought to Troy, thus starting the Trojan War.*

   Oenon's death: *Oenone stabbed herself, after the death of Paris.*

28 he, that built the walls of Thebes: *according to Greek mythology, Amphion played his harp with such skill that stones rose of their own accord to form the walls of Thebes.*

## Scene two

*Enter* FAUSTUS *in his study and* MEPHOSTOPHILIS.

FAUSTUS  When I behold the heavens, then I repent
  And curse thee, wicked Mephostophilis,
  Because thou hast depriv'd me of those joys.

MEPHOSTOPHILIS  'Twas thine own seeking, Faustus, thank
    thyself.
  But think'st thou heaven is such a glorious thing?
  I tell thee, Faustus, it is not half so fair
  As thou or any man that breathes on earth.

FAUSTUS  How prov'st thou that?

MEPHOSTOPHILIS  'Twas made for man; then he's more
    excellent.

FAUSTUS  If heaven was made for man, 'twas made for me     10
  I will renounce this magic and repent.

*Enter the two* Angels.

GOOD ANGEL  Faustus, repent; yet God will pity thee.

BAD ANGEL  Thou art a spirit; God cannot pity thee.

FAUSTUS  Who buzzeth in mine ears I am a spirit?
  Be I a devil, yet God may pity me;
  Yea, God will pity me if I repent.

BAD ANGEL  Ay, but Faustus never shall repent.

*Exeunt* Angels.

FAUSTUS  My heart is harden'd, I cannot repent.
  Scarce can I name salvation, faith, or heaven,
  But fearful echoes thunders in mine ears,     20
  'Faustus, thou art damn'd!' Then guns and knives,
  Swords, poison, halters, and envenom'd steel
  Are laid before me to dispatch myself;
  And long ere this I should have done the deed
  Had not sweet pleasure conquer'd deep despair.
  Have not I made blind Homer sing to me
  Of Alexander's love and Oenon's death?
  And hath not he, that built the walls of Thebes
  With ravishing sound of his melodious harp,

35 are there many spheres above the moon?: *the Elizabethans believed that the earth was the centre of the universe. The other heavenly bodies were set in 'spheres', which revolved around the earth. The nearest was the sphere of the moon, and Mephostophilis confirms to Faustus that beyond this sphere lie the spheres of six other 'erring stars' or planets: Mercury, Venus, the Sun, Mars, Jupiter, Saturn. Beyond this is the eighth sphere: the 'firmament', or sphere of the fixed stars. The ninth sphere is the 'empyreal orb', or 'heaven', made of fire and immovable.*

37 centric: *central.*

38 As are the elements . . . heavens: *Mephostophilis explains that just as the four elements enclose each other (earth is surrounded by water, water by air, and air by fire), so each sphere is circled by those beyond it.*

42 termine: *boundary; extremity.*

43–44 Nor are the names . . . feigned: *Mephostophilis says that it is not wrong to give the planets ('erring stars') individual names, since they each occupy separate spheres.*

45 situ et tempore: (Latin) *'in position and in time'. Faustus is asking whether all planets move at the same speed and in the same direction.*

48 the poles of the zodiac: *the common axle on which all the spheres revolve. The planets have 'double motion' (line 51) because although each rotates daily from east to west, they are also occupied individually with travelling (at their own, much slower and separate pace) from west to east.*

49 slender: *insubstantial; simple.*

56 freshman's suppositions: *elementary assumptions, taught to first-year undergraduates.*

57 intelligentia: (Latin) *spirit. It was believed that each planet was guided by an angelic spirit.*

62 coelum igneum? et crystallinum?: (Latin) *a fiery sphere? and a sphere of crystal [beyond God's heaven]?*

Made music with my Mephostophilis? 30
Why should I die, then, or basely despair?
I am resolv'd Faustus shall not repent. –
Come, Mephostophilis, let us dispute again,
And reason of divine astrology.
Speak, are there many spheres above the moon?
Are all celestial bodies but one globe
As is the substance of this centric earth?

MEPHOSTOPHILIS As are the elements, such are the
heavens,
Even from the moon unto the empyreal orb,
Mutually folded in each other's spheres, 40
And jointly move upon one axle-tree,
Whose termine is term'd the world's wide pole;
Nor are the names of Saturn, Mars, or Jupiter
Feign'd, but are erring stars.

FAUSTUS                              But have they all
One motion, both *situ et tempore*?

MEPHOSTOPHILIS All move from east to west in four-and-
twenty hours upon the poles of the world, but differ in
their motions upon the poles of the zodiac.

FAUSTUS These slender questions Wagner can decide:
Hath Mephostophilis no greater skill? 50
Who knows not the double motion of the planets?
That the first is finish'd in a natural day;
The second thus: Saturn in thirty years,
Jupiter in twelve, Mars in four, the sun, Venus, and
Mercury in a year, the moon in twenty-eight days.
These are freshmen's suppositions. But tell me, hath ev-
ery sphere a dominion or *intelligentia*?

MEPHOSTOPHILIS Ay.

FAUSTUS How many heavens or spheres are there?

MEPHOSTOPHILIS Nine: the seven planets, the firmament, 60
and the empyreal heaven.

FAUSTUS But is there not *coelum igneum*? *et crystallinum*?

MEPHOSTOPHILIS No, Faustus, they be but fables.

65 conjunctions: *apparent proximity of heavenly bodies.*
   oppositions: *extreme apparent divergence of heavenly bodies.*
   aspects: *the relative positions of heavenly bodies.*
68 per ... totius: (Latin) '*on account of their unequal motion relative
   to the whole*'. *In other words, the heavenly bodies move at different
   speeds.*

72 Move: *anger.*

74 against our kingdom: *contrary to the interests of hell.*

77 this: *what I have just said.*

84 raze: *graze.*

86 Help ... soul: *echo of line 79.*

88 interest in the same: *legal claim upon it.*

93 injure: *wrong.*

FAUSTUS  Resolve me then in this one question:
  Why are not conjunctions, oppositions, aspects, eclipses
  all at one time, but in some years we have more, in some
  less?

MEPHOSTOPHILIS  *Per inaequalem motum respectu totius.*

FAUSTUS  Well, I am answered. Now tell me who made the
  world.

MEPHOSTOPHILIS  I will not.                                      70

FAUSTUS  Sweet Mephostophilis, tell me.

MEPHOSTOPHILIS  Move me not, Faustus.

FAUSTUS  Villain, have not I bound thee to tell me any
  thing?

MEPHOSTOPHILIS  Ay, that is not against our kingdom.
  This is. Thou art damn'd; think thou of hell.

FAUSTUS  Think, Faustus, upon God, that made the world.

MEPHOSTOPHILIS  Remember this!
*Exit.*

FAUSTUS  Ay, go, accursed spirit, to ugly hell!
  'Tis thou hast damn'd distressed Faustus' soul.
  Is't not too late?                                             80
*Enter the two* Angels.

BAD ANGEL  Too late.

GOOD ANGEL  Never too late, if Faustus will repent.

BAD ANGEL  If thou repent, devils will tear thee in pieces.

GOOD ANGEL  Repent, and they shall never raze thy skin.
*Exeunt* Angels.

FAUSTUS  O Christ, my saviour, my saviour,
  Help to save distressed Faustus' soul.
*Enter* LUCIFER, BEELZEBUB, *and* MEPHOSTOPHILIS.

LUCIFER  Christ cannot save thy soul, for he is just;
  There's none but I have interest in the same.

FAUSTUS  O, what art thou that look'st so terribly?

LUCIFER  I am Lucifer,                                           90
  And this is my companion prince in hell.

FAUSTUS  O Faustus, they are come to fetch thy soul.

BEELZEBUB  We are come to tell thee thou dost injure us.

96 dam: *mother*.

103 gratify: *reward*.

105 pastime: *entertainment*.

107 proper: *individual; authentic*.

110 Talk not ... creation: *like the mention of marriage (Act II, Scene I, lines 142–143), such talk is inappropriate in diabolical company.*

111 show: *pageant*.

114 soon: *immediately*.

115 Pride: *notably, the first sin is that by which Lucifer fell and that which is now governing Faustus himself.*

116 Ovid's flea: *a mediaeval Latin poem 'The song of the Flea' (wrongly attributed to Ovid) shows a lover envying the flea's free access to his lady's body.*

117 periwig: *small wig*.

120 wrought: *embroidered*.
    list: *please*.

122 cloth of arras: *tapestry, woven at Arras in Flanders and normally used for wall-hangings.*

125 of: *by*.

126 churl: *miser*.
    leather bag: *purse; money bag*.

48

LUCIFER  Thou call'st on Christ contrary to thy promise.

BEELZEBUB  Thou shouldst not think on God.

LUCIFER                                          Think on the devil.

BEELZEBUB  And his dam too.

FAUSTUS  Nor will I henceforth; pardon me in this.
　　And Faustus vows never to look to heaven,
　　Never to name God or to pray to him,
　　To burn his scriptures, slay his ministers,　　　　　100
　　And make my spirits pull his churches down.

LUCIFER  So shalt thou show thyself an obedient servant,
　　And we will highly gratify thee for it.

BEELZEBUB  Faustus, we are come from hell in person to
　　show thee some pastime. Sit down, and thou shalt be-
　　hold the Seven Deadly Sins appear to thee in their own
　　proper shapes and likeness.

FAUSTUS  That sight will be as pleasant to me as paradise
　　was to Adam the first day of his creation.

LUCIFER  Talk not of paradise or creation, but mark the　　110
　　show. Go, Mephostophilis, fetch them in.

*Enter the* SEVEN DEADLY SINS [*led by a* Piper].

BEELZEBUB  Now, Faustus, question them of their names
　　and dispositions.

FAUSTUS  That shall I soon. What art thou, the first?

PRIDE  I am Pride. I disdain to have any parents. I am like
　　to Ovid's flea; I can creep into every corner of a wench:
　　sometimes, like a periwig, I sit upon her brow; next, like
　　a necklace, I hang about her neck; then, like a fan of
　　feathers, I kiss her lips; and then, turning myself to a
　　wrought smock, do what I list. But fie, what a smell is　　120
　　here! I'll not speak another word, unless the ground be
　　perfumed and covered with cloth of arras.

FAUSTUS  Thou art a proud knave indeed. What art thou,
　　the second?

COVETOUSNESS  I am Covetousness, begotten of an old
　　churl in a leather bag; and, might I now obtain my
　　wish, this house, you and all, should turn to gold,

49

131–132 a chimney-sweeper and an oyster-wife: *hence, black and smelly.*

143 case: *pair.*
rapiers: *fine bladed swords.*

144 withal: *with.*

145 some of you shall be:. *one of you is sure to prove.*

149 bevers: *snacks*

153 Martlemas-beef: *Martlemas or St Martin's day (11 November) was the day on which livestock was traditionally killed, and salted to preserve it for winter.*

156 March-beer: *strong beer, brewed in March and matured for at least two years.*

157 progeny: *lineage.*

162 Heigh-ho!: *yawn*

that I might lock you safe into my chest. O my sweet
gold!

FAUSTUS  And what art thou, the third?                    130

ENVY  I am Envy, begotten of a chimney-sweeper and an
oyster-wife. I cannot read and therefore wish all books
burned. I am lean with seeing others eat. O, that there
would come a famine over all the world, that all might
die, and I live alone! then thou shouldst see how fat I'd
be. But must thou sit and I stand? Come down, with a
vengeance!

FAUSTUS  Out, envious wretch! But what art thou, the
fourth?

WRATH  I am Wrath. I had neither father nor mother; I     140
leaped out of a lion's mouth when I was scarce an hour
old, and ever since have run up and down the world
with these case of rapiers, wounding myself when I
could get none to fight withal. I was born in hell; and
look to it, for some of you shall be my father.

FAUSTUS  And what art thou, the fifth?

GLUTTONY  I am Gluttony. My parents are all dead, and
the devil a penny they have left me but a small pension,
and that buys me thirty meals a day and ten bevers – a
small trifle to suffice nature. I come of a royal pedigree:  150
my father was a gammon of bacon, and my mother was
a hogshead of claret wine; my godfathers were these,
Peter Pickled-herring and Martin Martlemas-beef. But
my godmother, O, she was a jolly gentlewoman, and
well beloved in every good town and city; her name was
Margery March-beer. Now, Faustus, thou hast heard
all my progeny; wilt thou bid me to supper?

FAUSTUS  No, I'll see thee hanged; thou wilt eat up all my
victuals.

GLUTTONY  Then the devil choke thee.                      160

FAUSTUS  Choke thyself, glutton! What art thou, the sixth?

SLOTH  Heigh-ho! I am Sloth. I was begotten on a sunny
bank, where I have lain ever since; and you have done

164 injury: *harm; wrong.*

170 ell: *forty five inches (114 cm).*
    stockfish: *dried codfish. Lechery is assessing – the proficiency of prospective lovers in terms of penis size, and stating her preference for virility over impotence.*

178 throughly: *thoroughly.*

181 chary: *carefully.*

s.d. several ways: *in different directions.*

1 look to the horses: *Robin is working as an ostler at an inn.*
2 again: *back. Robin clearly wishes to abandon his work for the moment in order to experiment with the book of magic he has stolen from Faustus.*
3 as't passes: *as beats everything.*

me great injury to bring me from thence: let me be carried thither again by Gluttony and Lechery. Heigh-ho!
I'll not speak a word more for a king's ransom.

FAUSTUS And what are you, Mistress Minx, the seventh
and last?

LECHERY Who, I, sir? I am one that loves an inch of raw
mutton better than an ell of fried stockfish, and the first      170
letter of my name begins with Lechery.

LUCIFER Away, to hell, away! On, piper!

*Exeunt the* Seven Sins [*and the* Piper].

FAUSTUS O, how this sight doth delight my soul!

LUCIFER But, Faustus, in hell is all manner of delight.

FAUSTUS O, might I see hell and return again safe, how
happy were I then!

LUCIFER Faustus, thou shalt; at midnight I will send for
thee.
    Meanwhile peruse this book and view it throughly,
    And thou shalt turn thyself into what shape thou wilt.

FAUSTUS Thanks, mighty Lucifer.                               180
    This will I keep as chary as my life.

LUCIFER Now, Faustus, farewell.

FAUSTUS Farewell, great Lucifer. Come, Mephostophilis.

*Exeunt omnes several ways.*


## Scene three

*Enter the* Clown [ROBIN].

ROBIN What, Dick, look to the horses there till I come
again. I have gotten one of Doctor Faustus' conjuring
books, and now we'll have such knavery as 't passes.

*Enter* DICK.

DICK What, Robin, you must come away and walk the
horses.

ROBIN I walk the horses! I scorn 't, 'faith, I have other
matters in hand; let the horses walk themselves and

8 A per se ... o: *Robin is reading aloud laboriously: 'A, by itself, spells a; t, h, e, spell the; o, by itself, spells o.'*

8–9 deny ... gorgon: *Robin is trying to read 'Demogorgon', named in Faustus's invocation in Act I, Scene III, line 18.*

11 'Snails: *By God's nails! (an oath).*

12 on't: *of it.*

13 presently: *at once.*

14 hostry: *inn, hostelry.*

15 That's like, 'faith!: *highly likely, indeed! (meant ironically).*

16 an: *if.*

   he'll conjure you: *he'll sort you out!*

18 on's: *on his.*

20 my mistress hath done it: *his wife has already given him horns (the sign of a deceived husband) by being unfaithful.*

23 matters: *affairs. Robin is suggesting that he himself has been the lover of their mistress but is too much of a gentleman to reveal it.*
   disposed: *inclined.*

25–26 in good sadness: *seriously.*

31 claret wine: *red wine from Bordeaux, in France.*
   sack: *strong Spanish wine, light in colour.*
   muscadine: *muscatel (strong sweet white wine).*
   malmsey: *another strong sweet wine (from Madeira).*
   whippincrust: *distortion of 'hippocras', a spiced wine named after Hippocrates, the 'Father of Medicine'.*

32 hold-belly-hold: *belly-full.*

*As at the opening of the play, the Chorus is introduced to describe details of time and place and to evoke dimensions of space that cannot easily be staged directly.*

54

they will. [*Reading*] *A per se, a; t, h, e, the; o per se, o; deny orgon, gorgon.* Keep further from me, O thou illiterate and unlearned ostler.                    10

DICK  'Snails, what hast thou got there, a book? Why, thou canst not tell ne'er a word on't.

ROBIN  That thou shalt see presently. Keep out of the circle, I say, lest I send you into the hostry with a vengeance.

DICK  That's like, 'faith! You had best leave your foolery, for an my master come he'll conjure you, 'faith.

ROBIN  My master conjure me! I'll tell thee what, an my master come here, I'll clap as fair a pair of horns on's head as e'er thou sawest in thy life.

DICK  Thou needest not do that, for my mistress hath done    20
it.

ROBIN  Ay, there be of us here that have waded as deep into matters as other men, if they were disposed to talk.

DICK  A plague take you! I thought you did not sneak up and down after her for nothing. But I prithee tell me in good sadness, Robin, is that a conjuring book?

ROBIN  Do but speak what thou'lt have me to do, and I'll do 't. If thou'lt dance naked, put off thy clothes, and I'll conjure thee about presently. Or if thou'lt go but to the tavern with me, I'll give thee white wine, red wine,    30
claret wine, sack, muscadine, malmsey, and whippin-crust, hold-belly-hold, and we'll not pay one penny for it.

DICK  O brave! prithee let's to it presently, for I am as dry as a dog.

ROBIN  Come, then, let's away.
*Exeunt.*


## Chorus one

*Enter the* CHORUS
CHORUS  Learned Faustus,

3 Jove: *used here – as elsewhere – to refer to God.*

4 Olympus: *according to Greek mythology, the mountain home of the Gods.*

8 tropics, zones, and quarters of the sky: *the two tropics (of Cancer and Capricorn) and the two polar circles form the four 'quarters' which divide our world into five 'zones'.*

9 From ... primum mobile: *The primum mobile (Latin: 'first moving thing') was the sphere giving movement to all the spheres that it enclosed. Marlowe identified it with the eight sphere (or 'firmament') – see notes on Act II, Scene II, line 35. This phrase therefore means that Faustus travelled from the lowest to the highest of the moving spheres. His journey remained, however, within 'this circumference' (line 11). He did not venture to the ninth sphere – the immovable 'empyreal orb' of heaven.*

17 hale: *draw.*

19 subtle: *rarefied.*

20 prove: *put to the test.*

cosmography: *the science that maps the general features of the universe.*

24 take some part of: *take part in; share in.*

25 this day: *the feast of St Peter is on 29 June.*

solemniz'd: *celebrated with great ceremony.*

To find the secrets of astronomy,
Graven in the book of Jove's high firmament,
Did mount him up to scale Olympus' top,
Where, sitting in a chariot burning bright
Drawn by the strength of yoked dragons' necks,
He views the clouds, the planets, and the stars,
The tropics, zones, and quarters of the sky,
From the bright circle of the horned moon
Even to the height of *primum mobile*;                    10
And, whirling round with this circumference
Within the concave compass of the pole,
From east to west his dragons swiftly glide
And in eight days did bring him home again.
Not long he stay'd within his quiet house
To rest his bones after his weary toil,
But new exploits do hale him out again,
And, mounted then upon a dragon's back,
That with his wings did part the subtle air,
He now is gone to prove cosmography,                     20
That measures coasts and kingdoms of the earth,
And as I guess will first arrive at Rome
To see the Pope and manner of his court
And take some part of holy Peter's feast,
The which this day is highly solemniz'd.
*Exit.*

2 Trier: *city in western Germany, situated in a valley surrounded by hills bearing grapes.*

4 lakes: *moats.*

6 coasting: *passing along the side of, skirting.*

7 the river Main fall into Rhine: *the two rivers merge at Mainz.*

9 Naples, rich Campania: *the identification of Campania with Naples is incorrect and appears also in Marlowe's source.*

11 straight forth: *in straight lines.*

12 Quarters: *plural verb, governed by 'streets'.*
   equivalents: *equal parts.*

13 Maro: *Publius Vergilius Maro was the full name of the Roman poet, Virgil (70–19 B.C), author of the* Aeneid. *He was buried at Naples. During the Middle Ages he acquired a reputation for magic powers, as is shown by the following two lines.*

15 Thorough: *through.*

17 sumptuous temple: *St Mark's Cathedral in Venice.*

23 erst: *just recently.*

28 privy: *private.*

# Act Three

*Scene one*

*Enter* FAUSTUS *and* MEPHOSTOPHILIS.

FAUSTUS  Having now, my good Mephostophilis,
Pass'd with delight the stately town of Trier,
Environ'd round with airy mountain-tops,
With walls of flint, and deep-entrenched lakes,
Not to be won by any conquering prince;
From Paris next, coasting the realm of France,
We saw the river Main fall into Rhine,
Whose banks are set with groves of fruitful vines;
Then up to Naples, rich Campania,
With buildings fair and gorgeous to the eye,                    10
Whose streets straight forth and pav'd with finest brick
Quarters the town in four equivalents.
There saw we learned Maro's golden tomb,
The way he cut, an English mile in length,
Thorough a rock of stone in one night's space.
From thence to Venice, Padua, and the rest,
In midst of which a sumptuous temple stands,
That threats the stars with her aspiring top,
Whose frame is pav'd with sundry colour'd stones
And roof'd aloft with curious work in gold.                     20
Thus hitherto hath Faustus spent his time.
But tell me now, what resting-place is this?
Hast thou, as erst I did command,
Conducted me within the walls of Rome?
MEPHOSTOPHILIS  I have, my Faustus, and for proof thereof
This is the goodly palace of the Pope,
And 'cause we are no common guests
I choose his privy chamber for our use.
FAUSTUS  I hope his Holiness will bid us welcome.

30 All's one: *it doesn't matter whether he will or not.*

34 underprop the groundwork: *support the foundation.*
35 stream: *river.*

37 lean: *bend; incline.*

39 Ponte Angelo: *this bridge was built in AD 135 by Hadrian. In actual fact, the castle stands upon the bank of the Tiber facing the bridge.*
40 passing: *extraordinarily.*
41 store: *abundance.*
   ordinance: *artillery.*
42 double cannons: *cannons of very large calibre.*
45 pyramides: *reference to the obelisk, which was actually brought from Egypt to Rome by the Emperor Caligula (AD 12–41).*
48–49 Styx ... Acheron ... Phlegethon: *according to Greek mythology, the three rivers of Hades, the underworld of the dead.*
51 situation: *lay-out; whole extent.*
   bright-splendent: *brilliantly magnificent.*

57 the Pope's triumphant victory: *the Pope has captured Bruno, the rival pope nominated by the Holy Roman Emperor, Charles V. Charles V ruled as Emperor of Germany from 1519 until his abdication in 1556. Marlowe's Pope, however, (although modelled in part on the twelfth-century Alexander III) is fictitious. Similarly, Raymond – King of Hungary – and Bruno himself appear to be wholly imaginary.*
62 dalliance: *play.*

MEPHOSTOPHILIS  All's one, for we'll be bold with his veni-
    son.                                                    30
    But now, my Faustus, that thou may'st perceive
    What Rome contains for to delight thine eyes,
    Know that this city stands upon seven hills
    That underprop the groundwork of the same:
    Just through the midst run flowing Tiber's stream,
    With winding banks that cut it in two parts,
    Over the which four stately bridges lean,
    That make safe passage to each part of Rome.
    Upon the bridge call'd Ponte Angelo
    Erected is a castle passing strong,                   40
    Where thou shalt see such store of ordinance
    As that the double cannons forg'd of brass
    Do match the number of the days contain'd
    Within the compass of one complete year;
    Beside the gates, and high pyramides
    That Julius Caesar brought from Africa.
FAUSTUS  Now, by the kingdoms of infernal rule,
    Of Styx, of Acheron, and the fiery lake
    Of ever-burning Phlegethon, I swear
    That I do long to see the monuments            50
    And situation of bright-splendent Rome.
    Come, therefore, let's away.
MEPHOSTOPHILIS  Nay, stay, my Faustus; I know you'd see
    the Pope
    And take some part of holy Peter's feast,
    The which in state and high solemnity
    This day is held through Rome and Italy
    In honour of the Pope's triumphant victory.
FAUSTUS  Sweet Mephostophilis, thou pleasest me:
    Whilst I am here on earth let me be cloy'd
    With all things that delight the heart of man.     60
    My four-and-twenty years of liberty
    I'll spend in pleasure and in dalliance,
    That Faustus' name, whilst this bright frame doth stand,

64 admired: *wondered at. This use of the word recurs in line 89.*

76 show: *pageant; procession.*

77 this proud Pope: *the Pope's peevish pride is a parody of Faustus's own arrogance – an irony which escapes him.*
   cunning: *skill. This use of the word recurs in line 81.*

79 triumphs: *spectacular processions.*

84 antics: *clowns; grotesques.*

86 beads: *rosary beads.*
   pates: *bald heads.*

s.d. crosiers: *crosses carried by bishops.*
   pillars: *portable pillars carried as symbols of the cardinals' dignity.*
   procession: *form of prayer or religious office sung in a formal procession.*

90 Saxon: *that is, from Saxony in Germany.*

91 Whilst ... ascends: *Pope Alexander III (1159–81) compelled the Emperor Frederick Barbarossa (1152–90) to stoop to him in this way. See lines 136 and 137.*

93 state: *throne*

May be admired through the furthest land.

MEPHOSTOPHILIS 'Tis well said, Faustus; come, then, stand
    by me

And thou shalt see them come immediately.

FAUSTUS Nay, stay, my gentle Mephostophilis,

And grant me my request, and then I go.

Thou know'st within the compass of eight days

We view'd the face of heaven, of earth, and hell.    70

So high our dragons soar'd into the air

That looking down the earth appear'd to me

No bigger than my hand in quantity.

There did we view the kingdoms of the world,

And what might please mine eye I there beheld.

Then in this show let me an actor be,

That this proud Pope may Faustus' cunning see.

MEPHOSTOPHILIS Let it be so, my Faustus, but first stay

And view their triumphs as they pass this way;

And then devise what best contents thy mind,    80

By cunning in thine art to cross the Pope

Or dash the pride of this solemnity,

To make his monks and abbots stand like apes

And point like antics at his triple crown,

To beat the beads about the friars' pates

Or clap huge horns upon the cardinals' heads,

Or any villainy thou canst devise,

And I'll perform it, Faustus. Hark, they come!

This day shall make thee be admir'd in Rome.

*Enter the* Cardinals *and* Bishops, *some bearing crosiers, some the pillars;* Monks *and* Friars *singing their procession. Then the* POPE *and* RAYMOND, KING OF HUNGARY, *with* BRUNO *led in chains.*

POPE ADRIAN Cast down our footstool.

RAYMOND                   Saxon Bruno, stoop,    90

Whilst on thy back his Holiness ascends

Saint Peter's chair and state pontifical.

BRUNO Proud Lucifer, that state belongs to me:

But thus I fall to Peter, not to thee.

s.d. flourish: *fanfare of trumpets.*

99–100 as the gods ... punish men: *the Pope is referring to the proverb, 'God comes with leaden [woollen] feet but strikes with iron hands'.*

104 consistory: *meeting-place of the papal senate.*

105 statutes decretal: *papal decrees.*

106 holy council held at Trent: *the Vatican Council which sat, with interruptions, from 1545 to 1563.*

107 synod: *general council.*

112 Lord Raymond – : *while the Pope talks privately with Raymond, Faustus (unseen) gives instructions to Mephostophilis.*

118 parley: *hold conference.*

125 let me have some right of law: *allow that I have some legal claim.*

126 I was ... Emperor: *this line refutes the Pope's charge (line 109) that Bruno has challenged his position 'without election'.*

POPE ADRIAN  To me and Peter shalt thou grovelling lie
 And crouch before the papal dignity:
 Sound trumpets, then, for thus Saint Peter's heir
 From Bruno's back ascends Saint Peter's chair.
*A flourish while he ascends.*
 Thus as the gods creep on with feet of wool
 Long ere with iron hands they punish men,     100
 So shall our sleeping vengeance now arise
 And smite with death thy hated enterprise.
 Lord Cardinals of France and Padua,
 Go forthwith to our holy consistory
 And read amongst the statutes decretal
 What, by the holy council held at Trent,
 The sacred synod hath decreed for him
 That doth assume the papal government
 Without election and a true consent.
 Away, and bring us word with speed.     110
1 CARDINAL  We go, my lord.
*Exeunt* Cardinal.
POPE ADRIAN  Lord Raymond –
FAUSTUS  Go, haste thee, gentle Mephostophilis,
 Follow the cardinals to the consistory,
 And, as they turn their superstitious books,
 Strike them with sloth and drowsy idleness;
 And make them sleep so sound that in their shapes
 Thyself and I may parley with this Pope,
 This proud confronter of the Emperor,
 And in despite of all his holiness     120
 Restore this Bruno to his liberty
 And bear him to the states of Germany.
MEPHOSTOPHILIS  Faustus, I go.
FAUSTUS            Dispatch it soon:
 The Pope shall curse that Faustus came to Rome.
*Exeunt* FAUSTUS *and* MEPHOSTOPHILIS.
BRUNO  Pope Adrian, let me have some right of law;
 I was elected by the Emperor.

129 excommunicate: *cut off from membership of the Roman Catholic Church.*

130 interdict: *officially debarred.*

131 society: *company.*

132 He grows ... authority: *ironically, of course, the Pope's words apply both to himself and to Faustus.*

136 progenitor: *predecessor. See note on line 57.*

139–142 'That Peter's ... basilisk': *the source of this quotation is the account of Frederick's humiliation in Foxe's* Acts and Monuments, *better known as 'Foxe's Book of Martyrs'.*

142 basilisk: *mythical reptile, reputed to kill with a glance.*

143 schismatic: *member of a splinter group that has separated itself from the Church.*

146 Pope Julius ... Sigismund: *fictional characters.*

154 keys: *symbolic of St Peter's keys. In* Matthew XVI: 19 *Jesus promised: 'I will give you the keys of the Kingdom of Heaven.'*

157 Resign: *unseal.*
 whatso: *whatever.*

160 light: *fall; descend.*

POPE ADRIAN We will depose the Emperor for that deed
And curse the people that submit to him;
Both he and thou shalt stand excommunicate
And interdict from church's privilege                           130
And all society of holy men.
He grows too proud in his authority,
Lifting his lofty head above the clouds,
And like a steeple overpeers the church.
But we'll pull down his haughty insolence;
And, as Pope Alexander, our progenitor,
Trod on the neck of German Frederick,
Adding this golden sentence to our praise,
'That Peter's heirs should tread on emperors
And walk upon the dreadful adder's back,                        140
Treading the lion and the dragon down,
And fearless spurn the killing basilisk',
So will we quell that haughty schismatic
And by authority apostolical
Depose him from his regal government.
BRUNO Pope Julius swore to princely Sigismund,
For him and the succeeding popes of Rome,
To hold the emperors their lawful lords.
POPE ADRIAN Pope Julius did abuse the church's rights,
And therefore none of his decrees can stand.                    150
Is not all power on earth bestow'd on us?
And therefore though we would we cannot err.
Behold this silver belt, whereto is fix'd
Seven golden keys fast seal'd with seven seals
In token of our sevenfold power from heaven,
To bind or loose, lock fast, condemn, or judge,
Resign or seal, or whatso pleaseth us.
Then he and thou and all the world shall stoop,
Or be assured of our dreadful curse
To light as heavy as the pains of hell.                         160
*Enter* FAUSTUS *and* MEPHOSTOPHILIS *like the cardinals.*

161 fitted: *prepared; dressed.*

167 presently: *at once. This use of the word recurs in line 198.*

170 In quittance of: *as a punishment for.*

176 lollards: *heretics; originally, the followers of John Wyclif (c. 1328–84).*

178 assent: *will.*

179 enforcement of: *compulsion from.*

183 straight: *immediately.*

186 to Ponte Angelo: *that is, to the castle standing by the bridge. See the note on line 39.*

187 enclose him fast: *lock him up.*

189 college: *official title for the body of cardinals forming the Pope's council.*

193: again: *to return.*

MEPHOSTOPHILIS Now tell me, Faustus, are we not fitted
    well?
FAUSTUS Yes, Mephostophilis, and two such cardinals
    Ne'er serv'd a holy pope as we shall do.
    But whilst they sleep within the consistory
    Let us salute his reverend Fatherhood.
RAYMOND Behold, my lord, the cardinals are return'd.
POPE ADRIAN Welcome, grave fathers, answer presently,
    What have our holy council there decreed
    Concerning Bruno and the Emperor,
    In quittance of their late conspiracy        170
    Against our state and papal dignity?
FAUSTUS Most sacred patron of the church of Rome,
    By full consent of all the synod
    Of priests and prelates, it is thus decreed:
    That Bruno and the German Emperor
    Be held as lollards and bold schismatics
    And proud disturbers of the church's peace.
    And if that Bruno by his own assent,
    Without enforcement of the German peers,
    Did seek to wear the triple diadem        180
    And by your death to climb Saint Peter's chair,
    The statutes decretal have thus decreed,
    He shall be straight condemn'd of heresy
    And on a pile of faggots burnt to death.
POPE ADRIAN It is enough. Here, take him to your charge
    And bear him straight to Ponte Angelo,
    And in the strongest tower enclose him fast.
    Tomorrow, sitting in our consistory
    With all our college of grave cardinals,
    We will determine of his life or death.        190
    Here, take his triple crown along with you
    And leave it in the church's treasury.
    Make haste again, my good lord cardinals,
    And take our blessing apostolical.
MEPHOSTOPHILIS So, so; was never devil thus blest before.

199 solemnize: *celebrate in due form (as in Act II, Scene III, line 25).*

3 censure: *pass judgement upon.*
 posted: *conveyed swiftly.*

8 his crown: *the 'triple crown' which the Pope had ordered Faustus and Mephostophilis (in their disguise as cardinals) to deposit in the Church's treasury (Act III, Scene I, line 191).*

14 presently: *at once.*

20 the Furies' forked hair: *the Furies were the avenging spirits in Greek tragedy. Their hair consisted of snakes – to whose tongues the word 'forked' refers.*

FAUSTUS  Away, sweet Mephostophilis, be gone:
    The cardinals will be plagu'd for this anon.
*Exeunt* FAUSTUS *and* MEPHOSTOPHILIS [*with* BRUNO].
POPE ADRIAN  Go presently and bring a banquet forth,
    That we may solemnize Saint Peter's feast
    And with Lord Raymond, King of Hungary,        200
    Drink to our late and happy victory.
*Exeunt.*


## Scene two

*The banquet is brought in; and then enter* FAUSTUS *and*
MEPHOSTOPHILIS *in their own shapes.*
MEPHOSTOPHILIS  Now, Faustus, come, prepare thyself for
      mirth:
    The sleepy cardinals are hard at hand
    To censure Bruno, that is posted hence,
    And on a proud-pac'd steed as swift as thought
    Flies o'er the Alps to fruitful Germany,
    There to salute the woeful Emperor.
FAUSTUS  The Pope will curse them for their sloth today,
    That slept both Bruno and his crown away.
    But now, that Faustus may delight his mind
    And by their folly make some merriment,        10
    Sweet Mephostophilis, so charm me here
    That I may walk invisible to all
    And do whate'er I please, unseen of any.
MEPHOSTOPHILIS  Faustus, thou shalt; then kneel down
      presently,
    *Whilst on thy head I lay my hand*
    *And charm thee with this magic wand.*
    *First wear this girdle, then appear*
    *Invisible to all are here:*
    *The planets seven, the gloomy air,*
    *Hell, and the Furies' forked hair,*        20

21 Pluto's blue fire: *the sulphurous flames of hell. Pluto was the god of the underworld in classical mythology.*
Hecate's tree: *Hecate was goddess of the infernal region – queen of the night and guardian of witches. She was also Trivia, goddess of cross-roads where the gallows was set up, and it is probably to this that this phrase alludes.*

s.d. sennet: *trumpet fanfare.*

38 determine of: *decide.*

47 reserv'd: *kept safe.*

49 AMBO: *both.*
52 Hale: *drag.*
lade: *load.*
gyves: *chains.*

*Pluto's blue fire, and Hecate's tree*
*With magic spells so compass thee*
*That no eye may thy body see.*
So, Faustus, now, for all their holiness,
Do what thou wilt, thou shalt not be discern'd.

FAUSTUS Thanks, Mephostophilis; now, friars, take heed
Lest Faustus make your shaven crowns to bleed.

MEPHOSTOPHILIS Faustus, no more; see where the cardinals come.

*Sound a sennnet. Enter* POPE *and all the* Lords. *Enter the* Cardinals
*with a book.*

POPE ADRIAN Welcome, lord cardinals; come, sit down.
Lord Raymond, take your seat. Friars, attend,          30
And see that all things be in readiness,
As best beseems this solemn festival.

1 CARDINAL First, may it please your sacred Holiness
To view the sentence of the reverend synod
Concerning Bruno and the Emperor?

POPE ADRIAN What needs this question? Did I not tell you
Tomorrow we would sit i' th' consistory
And there determine of his punishment?
You brought us word even now, it was decreed
That Bruno and the cursed Emperor          40
Were by the holy council both condemn'd
For loathed lollards and base schismatics:
Then wherefore would you have me view that book?

1 CARDINAL Your Grace mistakes; you gave us no such
charge.

RAYMOND Deny it not; we all are witnesses
That Bruno here was late deliver'd you,
With his rich triple crown to be reserv'd
And put into the church's treasury.

AMBO CARD By holy Paul, we saw them not.

POPE ADRIAN By Peter, you shall die,          50
Unless you bring them forth immediately.
Hale them to prison, lade their limbs with gyves!

56 frolic: *playful*.

59 Fall to ... spare!: *Start eating, and may the devil choke you if you hold back!*

61 like: *please*.

62 beholding: *indebted*.

68 Was: *which was*.

73 adry: *thirsty*.

75 pledge: *drink a toast to*.

76 lubbers: *clumsy fellows*.

78 by our sanctitude: *note the irony that the Pope invokes his holy office as an excuse to dispose of personal enemies. He is not an exponent of Christian charity, despite his position as head of the Church.*

83 pardon: *indulgence (to pardon sins)*.

False prelates, for this hateful treachery
Curs'd be your souls to hellish misery.

[*Exeunt* Attendants *with the two* Cardinals.]

FAUSTUS  So, they are safe. Now, Faustus, to the feast:
The Pope had never such a frolic guest.

POPE ADRIAN  Lord Archbishop of Rheims, sit down with
us.

ARCHBISHOP  I thank your Holiness.

FAUSTUS  Fall to, the devil choke you an you spare!

POPE ADRIAN  Who's that spoke? Friars, look about.          60

FRIAR  Here's nobody, if it like your Holiness.

POPE ADRIAN  Lord Raymond, pray fall to: I am beholding
To the Bishop of Milan for this so rare a present.

FAUSTUS  I thank you, sir.

*Snatch it.*

POPE ADRIAN  How now! Who snatch'd the meat from me?
Villains, why speak you not? –
My good Lord Archbishop, here's a most dainty dish
Was sent me a cardinal in France.

FAUSTUS  I'll have that too.

[*Snatch it.*]

POPE ADRIAN  What lollards do attend our Holiness          70
That we receive such great indignity?
Fetch me some wine.

FAUSTUS  Ay, pray do, for Faustus is adry.

POPE ADRIAN  Lord Raymond, I drink unto your Grace.

FAUSTUS  I pledge your Grace.

[*Snatch it.*]

POPE ADRIAN  My wine gone too? Ye lubbers, look about
And find the man that doth this villainy,
Or by our sanctitude you all shall die. –
I pray, my lords, have patience at this
Troublesome banquet.                                        80

ARCHBISHOP  Please it your Holiness, I think it be
Some ghost crept out of purgatory, and now
Is come unto your Holiness for his pardon.

85 dirge: *requiem mass.*
86 lay: *calm.*

91 aware: *beware.*

95 this soul: *that is, the 'ghost crept out of purgatory' (line 82) who the Archbishop suggested might be trying to attract the Pope's attention to crave a pardon.*

97 cursed with bell, book, and candle: *this refers to a form of excommunication at the end of which the bell was tolled, the book closed, and the candle extinguished.*

104 Maledicat Dominus!: (Latin) *'May the Lord curse him.'*

107 took: *gave. Presumably this blow is delivered during the chanting itself.*

POPE ADRIAN It may be so:
  Go, then, command our priests to sing a dirge
  To lay the fury of this same troublesome ghost. –
  Once again, my lord, fall to.
*The* Pope *crosseth himself.*
FAUSTUS How now?
  Must every bit be spiced with a cross?
  Well, use that trick no more, I would advise you.          90
*Cross again.*
  Well, there's the second time; aware the third:
  I give you fair warning.
*Cross again.*
                                    Nay, then, take that!
FAUSTUS *hits him a box of the ear.*
POPE ADRIAN O, I am slain! help me, my lords;
  O, come and help to bear my body hence.
  Damn'd be this soul for ever for this deed.
*Exeunt the* Pope *and his train.*
MEPHOSTOPHILIS Now, Fautus, what will you do now? for
  I can tell you you'll be cursed with bell, book, and
  candle.
FAUSTUS Bell, book, and candle; candle, book, and bell;
  Forward and backward, to curse Faustus to hell!          100
*Enter the* Friars, *with bell, book, and candle, for the dirge.*
1 FRIAR Come, brethren, let's about our business with
  good devotion.
*Sing this.*
    *Cursed be he that stole his Holiness' meat from the table.*
      *Maledicat Dominus!*
    *Cursed be he that struck his Holiness a blow on the face.*
      *Maledicat Dominus!*
    *Cursed be he that took Friar Sandelo a blow on the pate.*
      *Maledicat Dominus!*
    *Cursed be he that disturbeth our holy dirge.*
      *Maledicat Dominus!*                                   110
    *Cursed be he that took away his Holiness' wine.*

113 Et omnes sancti!: (Latin) *And all the saints!*

1 we were ... answer: *we had better make sure that your devil can justify.*
2 stealing of this same cup: *note the way in which the street comedy is parodying the main action. In the previous scene, Faustus snatched a goblet (Act III, Scene II, line 75).*
   vintner: *innkeeper selling wine.*
   boy: *servant.*
3 at the hard heels: *right at our heels; close behind.*
4 An: *if.*
8 cunning: *skill.*

10 companions: *fellows.*

    *Maledicat Dominus!*
     *Et omnes sancti! Amen.*

[FAUSTUS *and* MEPHOSTOPHILIS] *beat the* Friars, *and fling fireworks among them, and so exeunt.*

## Scene three

*Enter* Clown [ROBIN] *and* DICK *with a cup.*

DICK Sirrah Robin, we were best look that your devil can
    answer the stealing of this same cup, for the vintner's boy
    follows us at the hard heels.

ROBIN 'Tis no matter, let him come! An he follows us, I'll
    so conjure him as he was never conjured in his life, I
    warrant him. Let me see the cup.

*Enter* VINTNER.

DICK Here 'tis. Yonder he comes. Now, Robin, now or
    never show thy cunning.

VINTNER O, are you here? I am glad I have found you.
    You are a couple of fine companions! Pray, where's the     10
    cup you stole from the tavern?

ROBIN How, how? we steal a cup! Take heed what you
    say; we look not like cup-stealers, I can tell you.

VINTNER Never deny't, for I know you have it, and I'll
    search you.

ROBIN Search me? Ay, and spare not. [*Aside to Dick*] Hold
    the cup, Dick. [*To the Vintner*] Come, come, search me,
    search me.

[Vintner *searches him.*]

VINTNER [*To Dick*] Come on, sirrah, let me search you
    now.     20

DICK Ay, ay, do, do. [*Aside to Robin*] Hold the cup, Robin.
    [*To the Vintner*] I fear not your searching; we scorn to
    steal your cups, I can tell you.

[Vintner *searches him.*]

24 Never outface ... matter: *don't try to brazen it out with me.*

26 beyond us both: *out of our hands. They have succeeded in juggling the cup so that neither holds it.*

29 Ay ... tell?: *derisive comments.*

30 circle: *that is, a magician's circle.*

31 say nothing: *it was dangerous to speak in the presence of spirits, according to tradition.*

32 O per se, o; Demogorgon: *Robin's reading is now a little more fluent than in Act II, Scene III, line 8.*
   Belcher: *one of the devils summoned by Wagner in Act I, Scene IV, line 34.*

36 From Constantinople ... now: *this is inconsistent with Mephostophilis's previous claim to Faustus that he 'came hither of (his) own accord' (Act I, Scene III, line 44), and strongly suggests therefore that this scene was not written by Marlowe himself.*

38 shrewd: *tiresome.*

39 a shoulder of mutton: *ironic reversal of Wagner's comment about Robin in Act I, Scene IV: 'he would give his soul to the devil for a shoulder of mutton' (lines 9–10).*

40 tester: *sixpence (a slang term).*

45 apish: *foolish.*

46 brave: *fine; marvellous.*

51 presently: *at once.*

54 wing myself: *make wings for myself.*
   amain: *at full speed.*

VINTNER  Never outface me for the matter, for sure the cup
is between you two.

ROBIN  Nay, there you lie; 'tis beyond us both.

VINTNER  A plague take you! I thought 'twas your knavery
to take it away. Come, give it me again.

ROBIN  Ay, much! when, can you tell? Dick, make me a
circle, and stand close at my back, and stir not for thy     30
life. Vintner, you shall have your cup anon. Say nothing, Dick. *O per se, o; Demogorgon, Belcher, and Mephostophilis!*

*Enter* MEPHOSTOPHILIS.

MEPHOSTOPHILIS  You princely legions of infernal rule,
How am I vexed by these villains' charms!
From Constantinople have they brought me now
Only for pleasure of these damned slaves.

[*Exit* Vintner.]

ROBIN  By lady, sir, you have had a shrewd journey of it.
Will it please you to take a shoulder of mutton to supper, and a tester in your purse, and go back again?          40

DICK  Ay, I pray you heartily, sir; for we called you but in
jest, I promise you.

MEPHOSTOPHILIS  To purge the rashness of this cursed
deed,
First be thou turned to this ugly shape,
For apish deeds transformed to an ape.

ROBIN  O brave, an ape! I pray, sir, let me have the carrying of him about to show some tricks.

MEPHOSTOPHILIS  And so thou shalt: by thou transformed
to a dog, and carry him upon thy back. Away, be gone!

ROBIN  A dog! that's excellent: let the maids look well to     50
their porridge-pots, for I'll into the kitchen presently.
Come, Dick, come.

*Exeunt the two* Clowns.

MEPHOSTOPHILIS  Now with the flames of ever-burning fire.
I'll wing myself and forthwith fly amain
Unto my Faustus, to the Great Turk's court.

*Exit.*

81

3 stay'd his course: *stopped his journeying.*
4 bare: *suffered.*
   but: *only.*
6 gratulate: *rejoice at.*
7 conference: *talk.*
   befell: *happened.*
9 of astrology: *on astronomy.*
11 wit: *understanding; learning.*

14 Carolus the Fifth: *the Emperor Charles V of Germany (1500–58).*
16 in trial of: *to demonstrate or experiment in.*

## Chorus two

*Enter* CHORUS.

CHORUS  When Faustus had with pleasure ta'en the view
    Of rarest things and royal courts of kings,
    He stay'd his course and so returned home,
    Where such as bare his absence but with grief –
    I mean his friends and nearest companions –
    Did gratulate his safety with kind words;
    And in their conference of what befell
    Touching his journey through the world and air
    They put forth questions of astrology,
    Which Faustus answer'd with such learned skill        10
    As they admir'd and wonder'd at his wit.
    Now is his fame spread forth in every land:
    Amongst the rest the Emperor is one,
    Carolus the Fifth, at whose palace now
    Faustus is feasted 'mongst his noblemen.
    What there he did in trial of his art
    I leave untold, your eyes shall see perform'd.

*Exit.*

2 Hie: *hasten; hurry.*
  presence: *audience chamber.*
3 voided straight: *emptied immediately.*
5 state: *throne.*

7 post: *in haste.*

10 fame: *glory.*

13 progenitors: *ancestors.*

15 warlike: *heroic.*
  semblances: *appearances.*
16 Alexander: *Alexander the Great, King of Macedon (356–323 BC).*
  paramour: *lover; probably a reference to Alexander's wife, Roxane, daughter of the Bactrian chief, Oxyartes, whose fortress Alexander captured.*
18 took his rouse: *had a heavy drinking session.*
  stoups: *measures.*
21 ope: *open.*
s.d. buttoning: *Benvolio has been roused from sleep. He is buttoning up his clothes.*
23 What . . . you two?: *What the devil's the matter with you two?*

# Act Four

## Scene one

*Enter* MARTINO *and* FREDERICK *at several doors.*

MARTINO  What ho, officers, gentlemen!
Hie to the presence to attend the Emperor.
Good Frederick, see the rooms be voided straight,
His Majesty is coming to the hall;
Go back, and see the state in readiness.

FREDERICK  But where is Bruno, our elected Pope,
That on a fury's back came post from Rome?
Will not his Grace consort the Emperor?

MARTINO  O yes, and with him comes the German con-
    juror,
The learned Faustus, fame of Wittenberg,          10
The wonder of the world for magic art;
And he intends to show great Carolus
The race of all his stout progenitors,
And bring in presence of his Majesty
The royal shapes and warlike semblances
Of Alexander and his beauteous paramour.

FREDERICK  Where is Benvolio?

MARTINO                  Fast asleep, I warrant you.
He took his rouse with stoups of Rhenish wine
So kindly yesternight to Bruno's health
That all this day the sluggard keeps his bed.       20

FREDERICK  See, see his window's ope; we'll call to him.

MARTINO  What ho, Benvolio!

*Enter* BENVOLIO *above at a window, in his nightcap, buttoning.*

BENVOLIO  What a devil ail you two?

MARTINO  Speak softly, sir, lest the devil hear you;
For Faustus at the court is late arriv'd,
And at his heels a thousand furies wait
To accomplish whatsoever the doctor please.

31 the Pope: *here, of course, this refers to Bruno.*
32 was: *this verb is plural in effect, governed by 'exploits'.*

36 post: *hasten.*
37 sport: *entertainment.*

39 and: *if.*

41 compass'd: *brought about.*

46 control: *overpower.*

4 professed: *declared.*
5 excellence: *dignity.*

BENVOLIO  What of this?

MARTINO  Come, leave thy chamber first, and thou shalt
   see
   This conjuror perform such rare exploits                    30
   Before the Pope and royal Emperor
   As never yet was seen in Germany.

BENVOLIO  Has not the Pope enough of conjuring yet?
   He was upon the devil's back late enough;
   And if he be so far in love with him
   I would he would post with him to Rome again.

FREDERICK  Speak, wilt thou come and see this sport?

BENVOLIO                                          Not I.

MARTINO  Wilt thou stand in thy window and see it then?

BENVOLIO  Ay, and I fall not asleep i'th' meantime.

MARTINO  The Emperor is at hand, who comes to see         40
   What wonders by black spells may compass'd be.

BENVOLIO  Well, go you attend the Emperor. I am content
   for this once to thrust my head out at a window, for they
   say if a man be drunk overnight the devil cannot hurt
   him in the morning. If that be true, I have a charm in
   my head shall control him as well as the conjuror, I
   warrant you.

[*Exeunt* FREDERICK *and* MARTINO.]


## Scene two

*A sennet.* CHARLES *the* GERMAN EMPEROR, BRUNO [DUKE OF]
SAXONY, FAUSTUS, MEPHOSTOPHILIS, FREDERICK, MARTINO, *and*
Attendants. [BENVOLIO *remains at his window.*]

EMPEROR  Wonder of men, renown'd magician,
   Thrice-learned Faustus, welcome to our court.
   This deed of thine, in setting Bruno free
   From his and our professed enemy,
   Shall add more excellence unto thine art

9 redeem'd: *set free; saved.*

11 despite of chance: *in spite of the ill luck he has suffered.*

21 ebon: *ebony.*

22 hale: *drag.*

23 compass: *bring about.*

24 Blood!: *By God's blood! (an oath).*

26 costermonger: *someone who sells fruit, fish or other goods from a barrow in the street.*

27 late: *lately; recently.*

32 presently: *immediately. This use of the word recurs at line 39.*

38 an: *if.*

40 Zounds: *By God's wounds! (an oath).*

Than if by powerful necromantic spells
Thou couldst command the world's obedience.
For ever be belov'd of Carolus;
And if this Bruno thou hast late redeem'd
In peace possess the triple diadem     10
And sit in Peter's chair despite of chance,
Thou shalt be famous through all Italy
And honour'd of the German Emperor.

FAUSTUS These gracious words, most royal Carolus,
Shall make poor Faustus is his utmost power
Both love and serve the German Emperor
And lay his life at holy Bruno's feet.
For proof whereof, if so your Grace be pleas'd,
The doctor stands prepar'd by power of art
To cast his magic charms, that shall pierce through     20
The ebon gates of ever-burning hell
And hale the stubborn furies from their caves
To compass whatsoe'er your Grace commands.

BENVOLIO Blood! he speaks terribly. But, for all that, I do
not greatly believe him; he looks as like a conjuror as the
Pope to a costermonger.

EMPEROR Then, Faustus, as thou late didst promise us,
We would behold that famous conqueror,
Great Alexander, and his paramour
In their true shapes and state majestical     30
That we may wonder at their excellence.

FAUSTUS Your Majesty shall see them presently. –
Mephostophilis, away,
And with a solemn noise of trumpets' sound
Present before this royal Emperor
Great Alexander and his beauteous paramour.

MEPHOSTOPHILIS Faustus, I will.

*Exit* MEPHOSTOPHILIS.

BENVOLIO Well, master doctor, an your devils come not
away quickly, you shall have me asleep presently.
Zounds, I could eat myself for anger to think I have     40

42 governor: *tutor*.

43 anon: *very soon*.

48 in dumb silence: *this echoes Robin's warning to Dick (Act III, Scene III, lines 31–32).*

50 And: *if.*

52 Actaeon: *according to mythology, Actaeon was a hunter who came upon the goddess Diana and her nymphs bathing. He was punished for seeing her naked by being turned into a stag, and his own hounds tore him to pieces.*

s.d. DARIUS: *King of Persia who spent most of his short reign defending his empire against Alexander. After being conquered by Alexander he was then murdered by one of his own subordinates (in 331 BC).*

s.d. offering to go out: *as Alexander proposes to leave.*

s.d. state: *throne.*

s.d. stays: *stops.*

55 but: *only.*

substantial: *solid; made of real matter.*

58 compass'd: *embraced.*

64 prove that saying to be true: *test the truth of that claim.*

been such an ass all this while to stand gaping after the
devil's governor, and can see nothing.

FAUSTUS  I'll make you feel something anon, if my art fail
  me not. —
  My lord, I must forewarn your Majesty
  That when my spirits present the royal shapes
  Of Alexander and his paramour
  Your Grace demand no questions of the King,
  But in dumb silence let them come and go.

EMPEROR  Be it as Faustus please; we are content.

BENVOLIO  Ay, ay, and I am content too. And thou bring    50
  Alexander and his paramour before the Emperor, I'll be
  Actaeon and turn myself to a stag.

FAUSTUS  And I'll play Diana and send you the horns presently.

*Sennet. Enter at one door the* EMPEROR ALEXANDER, *at the other*
DARIUS; *they meet;* DARIUS *is thrown down;* ALEXANDER *kills him,*
*takes off his crown, and, offering to go out, his* paramour *meets him; he*
*embraceth her and sets* DARIUS' *crown upon her head; and coming back*
*both salute the* emperor, *who, leaving his state, offers to embrace them,*
*which* FAUSTUS *seeing suddenly stays him. Then trumpets cease and music*
*sounds.*

  My gracious lord, you do forget yourself;
  These are but shadows, not substantial.

EMPEROR  O, pardon me, my thoughts are ravish'd so
  With sight of this renowned Emperor
  That in mine arms I would have compass'd him.
  But, Faustus, since I may not speak to them
  To satisfy my longing thoughts at full,    60
  Let me this tell thee: I have heard it said
  That this fair lady, whilst she liv'd on earth,
  Had on her neck a little wart or mole;
  How may I prove that saying to be true?

FAUSTUS  Your Majesty may boldly go and see.

EMPEROR  Faustus, I see it plain,
  And in this sight thou better pleasest me

70 strange beast: *Benvolio has fallen asleep at his window and Faustus's magic has caused a pair of horns to sprout from his head, thus fulfilling his rash promise to 'be Actaeon' (lines 51–52). The horns prevent him from pulling his head back through the window, during the exchange that follows.*
   yon: *the one over there.*

79 A plaque upon you!: *Benvolio has not recognized the Emperor.*
80 I blame . . . to sleep much: *I don't much blame you for sleeping.*

84 and: *if.*
   hold: *remain fast.*
84–85 'tis . . . sufficiently: *it doesn't matter about your head, for it's well protected.*

91 cunning: *ability.*

94 straight resolv'd: *determined at once.*

97 shall: *which shall.*
98 footmanship: *skill in running.*

100 Belimote, Argiron, Asterote!: *three devils.*
101 Hold, hold!: *Stop, stop!*

Than if I gain'd another monarchy.

FAUSTUS Away, be gone!

*Exit* Show.

    See, see, my gracious lord, what strange beast is yon,    70
    that thrusts his head out at the window.

EMPEROR O, wondrous sight! See, Duke of Saxony,
    Two spreading horns most strangely fastened
    Upon the head of young Benvolio.

DUKE OF SAXONY What, is he asleep, or dead?

FAUSTUS He sleeps, my lord, but dreams not of his horns.

EMPEROR This sport is excellent: we'll call and wake him.
    What ho, Benvolio!

BENVOLIO A plague upon you! let me sleep awhile.

EMPEROR I blame thee not to sleep much, having such a    80
    head of thine own.

DUKE OF SAXONY Look up, Benvolio, 'tis the Emperor
    calls.

BENVOLIO The Emperor! where? O, zounds, my head!

EMPEROR Nay, and thy horns hold, 'tis no matter for thy
    head, for that's armed sufficiently.

FAUSTUS Why, how now, sir knight? what, hanged by the
    horns? This is most horrible. Fie, fie, pull in your head
    for shame, let not all the world wonder at you.

BENVOLIO Zounds, doctor, is this your villainy?

FAUSTUS O, say not so, sir: the doctor has no skill,    90
    No art, no cunning to present these lords
    Or bring before this royal Emperor
    The mighty monarch, warlike Alexander.
    If Faustus do it, you are straight resolv'd
    In bold Actaeon's shape to turn a stag.
    And therefore, my lord, so please your Majesty,
    I'll raise a kennel of hounds shall hunt him so
    As all his footmanship shall scarce prevail
    To keep his carcase from their bloody fangs.
    Ho, Belimote, Argiron, Asterote!    100

BENVOLIO Hold, hold! Zounds, he'll raise up a kennel of

102 anon: *directly; in a moment.*

105 entreat: *beg.*

107 injury: *wrong.*

109 injurious: *insulting.*

113 and: *if.*
114 cuckold-makers: *reference to the belief that cuckolds (deceived husbands) sprouted horns. See Act II, Scene III, line 20.*
    of: *on.*
115 o' this order: *in this manner.*
115–116 smooth faces and small ruffs: *beardless scholars in academic dress.*
116 an: *if.*
120 In recompense ... desert: *to give you the reward you have so richly deserved.*

4 let slip: *overlook.*
  injury: *wrong.*
5 groom: *rascal.*
  my wrongs: *how I have been insulted.*
6 gambols: *frolics; jests.*
  proudly: *insolently.*

devils, I think, anon. Good my lord, entreat for me.
'Sblood, I am never able to endure these torments.

EMPEROR  Then, good master doctor,
Let me entreat you to remove his horns;
He has done penance now sufficiently.

FAUSTUS  My gracious lord, not so much for injury done to
me, as to delight your Majesty with some mirth, hath
Faustus justly requited this injurious knight; which
being all I desire, I am content to remove his horns. –  110
Mephostophilis, transform him. – And hereafter, sir,
look you speak well of scholars.

BENVOLIO  [*Aside*] Speak well of ye! 'Sblood, and scholars
be such cuckold-makers to clap horns of honest men's
heads o' this order, I'll ne'er trust smooth faces and
small ruffs more. But, an I be not revenged for this,
would I might be turned to a gaping oyster and drink
nothing but salt water.

EMPEROR  Come, Faustus, while the Emperor lives,
In recompense of this thy high desert,  120
Thou shalt command the state of Germany
And live belov'd of mighty Carolus.

*Exeunt omnes.*


## Scene three

*Enter* BENVOLIO, MARTINO, FREDERICK, *and* Soldiers.

MARTINO  Nay, sweet Benvolio, let us sway thy thoughts
From this attempt against the conjuror.

BENVOLIO  Away, you love me not, to urge me thus.
Shall I let slip so great an injury,
When every servile groom jests at my wrongs
And in their rustic gambols proudly say,
'Benvolio's head was grac'd with horns today'?
O, may these eyelids never close again
Till with my sword I have that conjuror slain.

13 But: *unless.*
quit: *requite; repay. The same use of the word recurs in line 32.*
infamy: *insult.*
14 betide: *come.*
16 hie: *hasten.*
18 Close: *hidden.*
19 By this: *by this time.*

25 Who: *whoever.*

27 ponderous: *heavy.*

30 bide: *await.*
31 in place: *on the spot.*

33 Close, close!: *Keep still, keep still!*
34 his gown: *the gown presumably allows the actor to conceal his real head while holding up the false head referred to in the stage directions.*
35 peasant: *rascal.*
37 anon: *at once.*

If you will aid me in this enterprise, 10
Then draw your weapons and be resolute:
If not, depart: here will Benvolio die
But Faustus' death shall quit my infamy.

FREDERICK Nay, we will stay with thee, betide what may,
And kill that doctor if he come this way.

BENVOLIO Then, gentle Frederick, hie thee to the grove
And place our servants and our followers
Close in an ambush there behind the trees.
By this, I know, the conjuror is near:
I saw him kneel and kiss the Emperor's hand 20
And take his leave laden with rich rewards.
Then, soldiers, boldly fight; if Faustus die,
Take you the wealth, leave us the victory.

FREDERICK Come, soldiers, follow me unto the grove:
Who kills him shall have gold and endless love.

*Exit* FREDERICK *with the* Soldiers.

BENVOLIO My head is lighter than it was by th' horns,
But yet my heart's more ponderous than my head
And pants until I see that conjuror dead.

MARTINO Where shall we place ourselves, Benvolio?

BENVOLIO Here will we stay to bide the first assault. 30
O, were that damned hell-hound but in place,
Thou soon shouldst see me quit my foul disgrace.

*Enter* FREDERICK.

FREDERICK Close, close! the conjuror is at hand
And all alone comes walking in his gown;
Be ready then and strike the peasant down.

BENVOLIO Mine be that honour, then: now, sword, strike home;
For horns he gave, I'll have his head anon.

*Enter* FAUSTUS *with the false head.*

MARTINO See, see, he comes.

BENVOLIO                        No words; this blow ends all.
Hell take his soul, his body thus must fall. [*Strikes.*]

FAUSTUS O! 40

97

43 griefs: *mischiefs.*

46 Was this: *ironically, these speeches employ the same rhetorical for-*
   *mula as the most celebrated words in the play (Act V, Scene I, line*
   *99).*
   made: *which made.*

55 quittance of: *repayment for.*

57 yok'd: *held fast (as with a yoke).*

61 birchen: *made of birch twigs.*

65 policy: *trick; scheme.*

70 recompense: *make amends for.*
71–72 limited ... earth: *granted the fixed period of twenty four*
   *years to live.*

FREDERICK Groan you, master doctor?

BENVOLIO Break may his heart with groans. Dear
    Frederick, see,

  Thus will I end his griefs immediately.

MARTINO Strike with a willing hand. His head is off.

[*Strikes;* FAUSTUS' *head falls off.*]

BENVOLIO The devil's dead; the furies now may laugh.

FREDERICK Was this that stern aspect, that awful frown,

  Made the grim monarch of infernal spirits

  Tremble and quake at his commanding charms?

MARTINO Was this that damned head whose heart con-
    spir'd

  Benvolio's shame before the Emperor?            50

BENVOLIO Ay, that's the head, and here the body lies,

Justly rewarded for his villainies.

FREDERICK Come, let's devise how we may add more
    shame

  To the black scandal of his hated name.

BENVOLIO First, on his head, in quittance of my wrongs,

  I'll nail huge forked horns and let them hang

  Within the window where he yok'd me first,

  That all the world may see my just revenge.

MARTINO What use shall we put his beard to?

BENVOLIO We'll sell it to a chimney-sweeper: it will wear   60
  out ten birchen brooms, I warrant you.

FREDERICK What shall his eyes do?

BENVOLIO We'll put out his eyes, and they shall serve for
  buttons to his lips to keep his tongue from catching cold.

MARTINO An excellent policy. And now, sirs, having
  divided him, what shall the body do?

[FAUSTUS *gets up*.]

BENVOLIO Zounds, the devil's alive again!

FREDERICK Give him his head, for God's sake!

FAUSTUS Nay, keep it; Faustus will have heads and hands,

  Ay, all your hearts, to recompense this deed.       70

  Knew you not, traitors, I was limited

73 had you: *if you had.*
74 hew'd: *chopped.*
75 had: *would have. The same construction recurs in the following line.*
77 dally: *delay over.*
78 Asteroth, Belimoth: *both devils were also summoned in Act IV, Scene II, under the names Belimote and Asterote (line 100).*
79 horse: *carry; mount.*

82 Yet stay: *but wait.*

84 caitiff: *wretch.*

89 steepy: *precipitous; sheer.*

92 dispatch my charge: *carry out my order.*

94 He must ... drives: *well-known proverb.*

100 peasants: *rascals.*
101 remove: *move; change their places.*
102 bulwarks: *defence barriers.*

For four-and-twenty years to breathe on earth?
And had you cut my body with your swords,
Or hew'd this flesh and bones as small as sand,
Yet in a minute had my spirit return'd
And I had breath'd a man made free from harm.
But wherefore do I dally my revenge?
Asteroth, Belimoth, Mephostophilis!
*Enter* MEPHOSTOPHILIS *and other* Devils.
Go, horse these traitors on your fiery backs
And mount aloft with them as high as heaven;     80
Thence pitch them headlong to the lowest hell.
Yet stay, the world shall see their misery,
And hell shall after plague their treachery.
Go, Belimoth, and take this caitiff hence
And hurl him in some lake of mud and dirt;
Take thou this other, drag him through the woods,
Amongst the pricking thorns and sharpest briers,
Whilst with my gentle Mephostophilis
This traitor flies unto some steepy rock
That rolling down may break the villain's bones     90
As he intended to dismember me.
Fly hence, dispatch my charge immediately.
FREDERICK Pity us, gentle Faustus, save your lives!
FAUSTUS Away!
FREDERICK     He must needs go that the devil drives.
*Exeunt* Spirits *with the* Knights.
*Enter the ambushed* Soldiers.
1 SOLDIER Come, sirs, prepare yourselves in readiness,
Make haste to help these noble gentlemen;
I heard them parley with the conjuror.
2 SOLDIER See where he comes; dispatch, and kill the
slave.
FAUSTUS What's here? an ambush to betray my life!
Then, Faustus, try thy skill. Base peasants, stand!     100
For lo, these trees remove at my command
And stand as bulwarks 'twixt yourselves and me

105 incontinent: *without delay.*
s.d. the door: *that is, the door at the back of the stage.*
    ensign: *flag; standard.*
    divers: *several.*



s.d. several: *separate.*



 6 Benvolio's: *Benvolio has.*


 9 no power to kill: *Martino is punning on the words 'haunted' and 'hunted'. He says that he and Frederick are not equipped to hunt Benvolio to death.*


13 chafe: *fret.*
    sped: *done for.*
15 spite of spite: *despite everything.*

To shield me from your hated treachery:
Yet to encounter this your weak attempt
Behold an army comes incontinent.

FAUSTUS *strikes the door, and enter a* Devil *playing on a drum, after him another bearing an ensign, and divers with weapons;* MEPHOSTOPHILIS *with fireworks; they set upon the* Soldiers *and drive them out.*
[*Exit* FAUSTUS.]

## Scene four

*Enter at several doors* BENVOLIO, FREDERICK, *and* MARTINO, *their heads and faces bloody, and besmeared with mud and dirt, all having horns on their heads.*

MARTINO  What ho, Benvolio!
BENVOLIO                          Here! What, Frederick, ho!
FREDERICK  O help me, gentle friend. Where is Martino?
MARTINO  Dear Frederick, here,
  Half smother'd in a lake of mud and dirt,
  Through which the furies dragg'd me by the heels.
FREDERICK  Martino, see! Benvolio's horns again.
MARTINO  O misery! How now, Benvolio?
BENVOLIO  Defend me, heaven, shall I be haunted still?
MARTINO  Nay, fear not, man, we have no power to kill.
BENVOLIO  My friends transformed thus! O hellish spite,     10
  Your heads are all set with horns.
FREDERICK                          You hit it right:
  It is your own you mean, feel on your head.
BENVOLIO  Zounds, horns again!
MARTINO                Nay, chafe, not, man, we all are sped.
BENVOLIO  What devil attends this damn'd magician,
  That, spite of spite, our wrongs are doubled?
FREDERICK  What may we do that we may hide our
      shames?
BENVOLIO  If we should follow him to work revenge,

21 joining near: *adjacent to*.
22 repair: *go*.

24 Sith: *since*.
25 We'll ... shame: *variation on the proverb, 'it is better to die with honour than live with shame'*.

s.d. HORSE-COURSER: *horse-dealer. This profession had a reputation for dishonesty.*

10 stand: *haggle*.

13 in any case: *whatever happens*.
    not into the water: *traditionally, running water (but not the stagnant water of a ditch) dissolves a witch's spell.*
14–15 will he ... waters?: *will he not be ready to go anywhere?*

21 a made man: *man of means.*

He'd join long asses' ears to these huge horns
And make us laughing-stocks to all the world.

MARTINO  What shall we then do, dear Benvolio?                    20

BENVOLIO  I have a castle joining near these woods,
   And thither we'll repair and live obscure
   Till time shall alter these our brutish shapes.
   Sith black disgrace hath thus eclips'd our fame,
   We'll rather die with grief than live with shame.

*Exeunt omnes.*


## Scene five

*Enter* FAUSTUS *and the* HORSE-COURSER.

HORSE-COURSER  I beseech your worship, accept of these
   forty dollars.

FAUSTUS  Friend, thou canst not buy so good a horse for so
   small a price. I have no great need to sell him; but if
   thou likest him for ten dollars more, take him, because I
   see thou hast a good mind to him.

HORSE-COURSER  I beseech you, sir, accept of this. I am a
   very poor man and have lost very much of late by horse-
   flesh, and this bargain will set me up again.

FAUSTUS  Well, I will not stand with thee; give me the       10
   money. Now, sirrah, I must tell you that you may ride
   him o'er hedge and ditch and spare him not; but, do you
   hear? in any case ride him not into the water.

HORSE-COURSER  How, sir, not into the water? Why, will he
   not drink of all waters?

FAUSTUS  Yes, he will drink of all waters. But ride him not
   into the water; o'er hedge and ditch, or where thou wilt,
   but not into the water. Go, bid the ostler deliver him
   unto you; and remember what I say.

HORSE-COURSER  I warrant you, sir. O, joyful day! now am   20
   I a made man for ever.

*Exit.*

23 fatal time: *time allotted by fate.*

25 Confound: *disperse.*
   passions: *agitated feelings.*
26 call: *offer salvation to.*
27 in conceit: *in this thought.*

28 cozening: *cheating. The word recurs in line 33.*

33 again: *back.*
   scab: *scoundrel.*
35 bottle: *bundle.*

44 Faustus hath his leg again: *the leg pulled off by the horse dealer has been replaced by magic.*

49 provision fit: *all that is necessary.*

FAUSTUS  What art thou, Faustus, but a man condemn'd to
    die?
    Thy fatal time draws to a final end;
    Despair doth drive distrust into my thoughts.
    Confound these passions with a quiet sleep.
    Tush, Christ did call the thief upon the cross;
    Then rest thee, Faustus, quiet in conceit.

*He sits to sleep.*

*Enter the* HORSE-COURSER, *wet.*

HORSE-COURSER  O, what a cozening doctor was this! I,
    riding my horse into the water, thinking some hidden
    mystery had been in the horse, I had nothing under me          30
    but a little straw and had much ado to escape drowning.
    Well, I'll go rouse him and make him give me my forty
    dollars again. Ho, sirrah doctor, you cozening scab!
    Master doctor, awake, and rise, and give me my money
    again, for your horse is turned to a bottle of hay. Master
    doctor!

*He pulls off his leg.*

    Alas, I am undone! what shall I do? I have pulled off his
    leg.

FAUSTUS  O, help, help! the villain hath murdered me.

HORSE-COURSER  Murder or not murder, now he has but          40
    one leg I'll outrun him and cast this leg into some ditch
    or other.

*[Exit.]*

FAUSTUS  Stop him, stop him, stop him! – Ha, ha, ha!
    Faustus hath his leg again, and the horse-courser a bun-
    dle of hay for his forty dollars.

*Enter* WAGNER.

    How now, Wagner, what news with thee?

WAGNER  If it please you, the Duke of Vanholt doth
    earnestly entreat your company and hath sent some of
    his men to attend you with provision fit for your jour-
    ney.                                                          50

FAUSTUS  The Duke of Vanholt's an honourable gentle-

52–53 no niggard of my cunning: *no miser with my skill.*

s.d. CARTER: *someone who hires himself to carry goods, using a horse and cart.*

  2 Where be these whores?: *crude summons to the hostess and her staff.*

  7 on the score: *in debt.*

11–12 I hope my score stands still: *Robin means that he hopes his debt has not risen. The Hostess, however, applies 'still' in a different sense, to mean 'always'. Thus she retorts that he is permanently in debt since he is in no hurry to pay her.*

16 presently: *without delay.*

    Look up ... ho!: *the Hostess is calling to her servants.*

20 bravest: *finest.*

21 Fauster: *incorrect version of Faustus's name.*

22 Here's some on's have: *There are some of us here who have.*

25 t'other: *the other.*

man, and one to whom I must be no niggard of my
cunning. Come away!

*Exeunt.*

## Scene six

*Enter* Clown [ROBIN], DICK, HORSE-COURSER, *and a* CARTER.

CARTER Come, my masters, I'll bring you to the best beer
in Europe. What ho, hostess! Where be these whores?

*Enter* Hostess.

HOSTESS How now, what lack you? What, my old guests,
welcome.

ROBIN Sirrah Dick, dost thou know why I stand so mute?

DICK No, Robin, why is't?

ROBIN I am eighteen pence on the score. But say nothing;
see if she have forgotten me.

HOSTESS Who's this that stands so solemnly by himself?
What, my old guest!                                                    10

ROBIN O, hostess, how do you? I hope my score stands
still.

HOSTESS Ay, there's no doubt of that, for methinks you
make no haste to wipe it out.

DICK Why, hostess, I say, fetch us some beer.

HOSTESS You shall presently. Look up into th' hall there,
ho!

*Exit.*

DICK Come, sirs, what shall we do now till mine hostess
comes?

CARTER Marry, sir, I'll tell you the bravest tale how a con-                20
juror served me. You know Doctor Fauster?

HORSE-COURSER Ay, a plague take him! Here's some on's
have cause to know him. Did he conjure thee too?

CARTER I'll tell you how he served me. As I was going to
Wittenberg t'other day with a load of hay, he met me
and asked me what he should give me for as much hay

109

29 three-farthings: *three quarters of an old penny.*
   presently: *at once.*
30 cursen: *Christian; the dialectal form of 'christened'.*
31 eat: *eaten. This form recurs in the following two speeches.*
34 eat a load of logs: *apparently a reference to the waste or abuse of timber on a local estate.*

37 of: *from.*

42 quoth: *said.*

47 bottle: *bundle.*
48 brave: *excellent.*
49 bravely: *well.*

54 hostry: *inn. The horse dealer has clearly abandoned his plan to throw the leg 'into some ditch or other' (Act IV, Scene V, lines 41–42).*
57 the likeness of an ape's face: *this incident was related in Act III, Scene III, line 45.*

as he could eat. Now, sir, I, thinking that a little would
serve his turn, bade him take as much as he would for
three farthings. So he presently game me my money and
fell to eating; and, as I am a cursen man, he never left        30
eating till he had eat up all my load of hay.

ALL O monstrous, eat a whole load of hay!

ROBIN Yes, yes, that may be, for I have heard of one that
has eat a load of logs.

HORSE-COURSER Now, sirs, you shall hear how vil-
lainously he served me. I went to him yesterday to buy a
horse of him, and he would by no means sell him under
forty dollars. So, sir, because I knew him to be such a
horse as would run over hedge and ditch and never tire,
I gave him his money. So, when I had my horse, Doctor        40
Fauster bade me ride him night and day and spare him
no time. 'But,' quoth he, 'in any case ride him not into
the water.' Now, sir, I, thinking the horse had had some
rare quality that he would not have me know of, what
did I but rid him into a great river? and when I came
just in the midst my horse vanished away, and I sat
straddling upon a bottle of hay.

ALL O brave doctor!

HORSE-COURSER But you shall hear how bravely I served
him for it. I went me home to his house, and there I        50
found him asleep. I kept a hallooing and whooping in
his ears, but all could not wake him. I, seeing that, took
him by the leg and never rested pulling till I had pulled
me his leg quite off; and now 'tis at home in mine hostry.

DICK And has the doctor but one leg then? That's excellent, for one of his devils turned me into the likeness of
an ape's face.

CARTER Some more drink, hostess!

ROBIN Hark you, we'll into another room and drink        60
awhile, and then we'll go seek out the doctor.

*Exeunt omnes.*

111

2–3 **recompense your great deserts:** *reward you in the fine way you deserve.*

12 **great-bellied:** *pregnant.*
13 **are:** *that are.*

18 **meat:** *food.*

28 **circles:** *hemispheres. These 'two circles' would be the northern and southern hemispheres, but the author appears to be thinking in terms of east and west, which makes this account rather muddled.*

## Scene seven

*Enter the* DUKE OF VANHOLT, *his* DUCHESS, FAUSTUS, *and*
MEPHOSTOPHILIS.

DUKE OF VANHOLT Thanks, master doctor, for these
pleasant sights. Nor know I how sufficiently to recompense your great deserts in erecting that enchanted castle in the air, the sight whereof so delighted me, as
nothing in the world could please me more.

FAUSTUS I do think myself, my good lord, highly recom-
pensed in that it pleaseth your Grace to think but well of
that which Faustus hath performed. But, gracious lady,
it may be that you have taken no pleasure in those
sights; therefore I pray you tell me what is the thing you    10
most desire to have: be it in the world, it shall be yours.
I have heard that great-bellied women do long for
things are rare and dainty.

DUCHESS OF VANHOLT True, master doctor, and, since I
find you so kind, I will make known unto you what my
heart desires to have; and were it now summer, as it is
January, a dead time of the winter, I would request no
better meat than a dish of ripe grapes.

FAUSTUS This is but a small matter. Go, Mephostophilis,
away!

*Exit* MEPHOSTOPHILIS.

Madam, I will do more than this for your content.    20

*Enter* MEPHOSTOPHILIS *again with the grapes.*

Here, now taste ye these; they should be good,
For they come from a far country, I can tell you.

DUKE OF VANHOLT This makes me wonder more than all
the rest,
That at this time of the year, when every tree
Is barren of his fruit, from whence you had
These ripe grapes.

FAUSTUS Please it your Grace, the year is divided into two
circles over the whole world, so that, when it is winter

113

29 likewise: *in the same manner.*

30 Saba: *Sheba.*

s.d. bounce: *beat; knock loudly. The Clowns believe that they have simply entered 'another room', as they planned at the end of Act IV, Scene VI (line 60). Instead, however, Faustus has transported them by magic to the court of Vanholt.*

39 coil: *row; din.*

41 a fig for him!: *expression of contempt, presumably inspired by the implied pun on 'reason' and 'raisin'.*

42 varlets: *rascals.*

43 I hope, sir ... welcome: *the horse dealer is offended by the unfavourable reception he detects. He trusts that the Clowns will have the sense to behave with a boldness that will make up for their poor welcome.*

45 It appears so: *obviously. The servant remarks dryly that they are not at all welcome.*

49 Commit the rascals: *take the scoundrels to prison.*

50 Commit with us!: *because of the implications of 'commit' in phrases such as 'commit adultery', Dick thinks that the Duke has authorised a sexual assault!*

56 outrageous: *violent.*

with us, in the contrary circle it is likewise summer with
them, as in India, Saba, and such countries that lie far    30
east, where they have fruit twice a year. From whence,
by means of a swift spirit that I have, I had these grapes
brought as you see.

DUCHESS OF VANHOLT And, trust me, they are the sweetest
grapes that e'er I tasted.

*The* Clowns *bounce at the gate within.*

DUKE OF VANHOLT What rude disturbers have we at the
    gate?
  Go, pacify their fury, set it ope,
  And then demand of them what they would have.

*They knock again and call out to talk with* FAUSTUS.

A SERVANT Why, how now, masters, what a coil is there!
  What is the reason you disturb the Duke?    40

DICK We have no reason for it, therefore a fig for him!

SERVANT Why, saucy varlets, dare you be so bold?

HORSE-COURSER I hope, sir, we have wit enough to be
  more bold than welcome.

SERVANT It appears so: pray be bold elsewhere,
  And trouble not the Duke.

DUKE OF VANHOLT         What would they have?

SERVANT They all cry out to speak with Doctor Faustus.

CARTER Ay, and we will speak with him.

DUKE OF VANHOLT Will you, sir? Commit the rascals.

DICK Commit with us! He were as good commit with his    50
  father as commit with us.

FAUSTUS I do beseech your Grace, let them come in;
  They are good subject for a merriment.

DUKE OF VANHOLT Do as thou wilt, Faustus; I give thee
  leave.

FAUSTUS I thank your Grace.

*Enter the* Clown [ROBIN], DICK, CARTER, *and* HORSECOURSER.
        Why, how now, my good friends?
  'Faith, you are too outrageous; but come near,
  I have procur'd your pardons. Welcome all!

58 we will be welcome for our money: *Robin believes that they are in a tavern and insists that they will pay for their welcome.*

63 sir sauce-box: *name given to someone cheeky or impertinent.*

68 furious: *insistent.*

70 gage: *stake.*

78 forgot: *forgotten.*

80–81 stand much upon that: *(probably) attach much importance to that. However, since 'leg' could also mean 'bow' (as in the pun at line 92), the horse dealer could be commenting on Faustus's bad manners and saying that he does not stand on ceremony.*

82 not much upon a wooden leg: *Faustus uses the words in their literal sense to make a somewhat predictable joke.*

ROBIN  Nay, sir, we will be welcome for our money, and we
will pay for what we take. What ho! give's half-a-dozen
of beer here, and be hanged.                                    60

FAUSTUS  Nay, hark you, can you tell me where you are?

CARTER  Ay, marry, can I; we are under heaven.

SERVANT  Ay, but, sir sauce-box, know you in what place?

HORSE-COURSER  Ay, ay, the house is good enough to drink
in. Zounds, fill us some beer, or we'll break all the bar-
rels in the house and dash out all your brains with your
bottles.

FAUSTUS  Be not so furious; come, you shall have beer.
My lord, beseech you give me leave awhile;
I'll gage my credit, 'twill content your Grace.                 70

DUKE OF VANHOLT  With all my heart, kind doctor, please
thyself;
Our servants and our court's at thy command.

FAUSTUS  I humbly thank your Grace. Then fetch some
beer.

HORSE-COURSER  Ay, marry, there spake a doctor indeed;
and, 'faith, I'll drink a health to thy wooden leg for that
word.

FAUSTUS  My wooden leg! what dost thou mean by that?

CARTER  Ha, ha, ha! Dost hear him, Dick? He has forgot
his leg.

HORSE-COURSER  Ay, ay, he does not stand much upon       80
that.

FAUSTUS  No, 'faith, not much upon a wooden leg.

CARTER  Good Lord, that flesh and blood should be so frail
with your worship! Do not you remember a horse-
courser you sold a horse to?

FAUSTUS  Yes, I remember I sold one a horse.

CARTER  And do you remember you bid he should not ride
him into the water?

FAUSTUS  Yes, I do very well remember that.

CARTER  And do you remember nothing of your leg?         90

FAUSTUS  No, in good sooth.

92 curtsy: *bow. This request plays on the second meaning of 'leg'. See note to lines 80–81.*

93 I thank you, sir: *this remark is made ironically, to accompany a mocking bow.*

94 'Tis not so much worth: *Don't mention it.*

97 Be ... bedfellows?: *Do both of your legs sleep in the same bed?*

99 colossus: *gigantic statue. The Colossus at Rhodes was said, erroneously, to span the harbour with its legs. Faustus is asking whether the Carter is suggesting that his legs are capable of separating so widely.*

102 fain: *gladly.*

113: cozened: *cheated.*

116 whoreson: *insult – literally, 'son of a whore'.*
    scab: *scoundrel.*

118 carry it away: *carry it off; have the advantage.*

119 'hey-pass' and 're-pass': *jugglers' and conjurors' exclamations when commanding objects to move. A modern equivalent is 'hey presto'.*

121 Who pays for the ale?: *the ale was brought in at line 102.*

CARTER  Then I pray remember your curtsy.

FAUSTUS  I thank you, sir.

CARTER  'Tis not so much worth. I pray you tell me one
thing.

FAUSTUS  What's that?

CARTER  Be both your legs bedfellows every night
together?

FAUSTUS  Wouldst thou make a colossus of me, that thou
askest me such questions?                                    100

CARTER  No, truly, sir, I would make nothing of you; but I
would fain know that.

*Enter* HOSTESS *with drink.*

FAUSTUS  Then I assure thee certainly they are.

CARTER  I thank you, I am fully satisfied.

FAUSTUS  But wherefore dost thou ask?

CARTER  For nothing, sir; but methinks you should have a
wooden bedfellow of one of 'em.

HORSE-COURSER  Why, do you hear, sir, did not I pull off
one of your legs when you were asleep?

FAUSTUS  But I have it again now I am awake: look you    110
here, sir.

ALL  O horrible! Had the doctor three legs?

CARTER  Do you remember, sir, how you cozened me and
eat up my load of –

FAUSTUS *charms him dumb.*

DICK  Do you remember how you made me wear an ape's –
[FAUSTUS *charms him dumb.*]

HORSE-COURSER  You whoreson conjuring scab, do you remember how you cozened me with a ho –
[FAUSTUS *charms him dumb.*]

ROBIN  Ha' you forgotten me? You think to carry it away
with your 'hey-pass' and 're-pass'. Do you remember
the dog's fa –                                               120
[FAUSTUS *charms him dumb*]. *Exeunt* Clowns.

HOSTESS  Who pays for the ale? Hear you, master doctor,

126 beholding: *indebted*.

129 all sad thoughts away: *ironic comment in view of the fear and loneliness voiced by Faustus in Act IV, Scene V (lines 22–27). He can never wholly forget his fate.*

now you have a sent away my guests, I pray who shall
pay me for my a –

[FAUSTUS *charms her dumb*.] *Exit* Hostess.

DUCHESS OF VANHOLT  My lord,

We are much beholding to this learned man.

DUKE OF VANHOLT  So are we, madam, which we will recompense

With all the love and kindness that we may.

His artful sport drives all sad thoughts away.

*Exeunt*.

3 store: *abundant supply*.

4 ducats: *gold coins*.

6 carouse: *drink freely*.

7 even now: *at this very moment*.

8 belly-cheer: *gluttonous merry-making*.

11 conference: *discussion*.

13 determined with ourselves: *decided*.
   Helen of Greece: *Helen was married to the Greek prince Mene-laus, the brother of King Agamemnon. When Paris seduced her and carried her off to Troy, the Greeks began a war against the Trojans to reclaim her.*

16–17 peerless dame ... majesty: *these words anticipate lines 23–4 and 29.*

18 beholding: *obliged; indebted*.

20 For that: *because*.

24 otherways: *otherwise*.

25 Sir Paris: *Paris is here given a mediaeval title, which associates him with romance and chivalry.*

26 spoils: *booty (including Helen) acquired during his expedition to Sparta, where Menelaus was King.*
   Dardania: *city built by Dardanus on the Hellespont; but the name is often used, as here, to refer to Troy.*

27 Be silent ... words: *as at Act III, Scene III, lines 30–31 and Act IV, Scene II, line 48, watchers are warned not to speak in the presence of spirits.*

# Act Five

## *Scene one*

*Thunder and lightning. Enter* DEVILS *with covered dishes.*
MEPHOSTOPHILIS *leads them into* FAUSTUS' *study. Then enter* WAGNER.

WAGNER  I think my master means to die shortly:
    He has made his will and given me his wealth,
    His house, his goods, and store of golden plate,
    Besides two thousand ducats ready coin'd.
    I wonder what he means. If death were nigh,
    He would not banquet and carouse and swill
    Amongst the students, as even now he doth,
    Who are at supper with such belly-cheer
    As Wagner ne'er beheld in all his life.
    See where they come; belike the feast is ended.    10
*Exit.*

*Enter* FAUSTUS, MEPHOSTOPHILIS, *and two or three* SCHOLARS.

1 SCHOLAR  Master Doctor Faustus, since our conference
    about fair ladies, which was the beautifullest in all the
    world, we have determined with ourselves that Helen of
    Greece was the admirablest lady that ever lived. There-
    fore, master doctor, if you will do us that favour, as to
    let us see that peerless dame of Greece, whom all the
    world admires for majesty, we should think ourselves
    much beholding unto you.

FAUSTUS  Gentlemen,
    For that I know your friendship is unfeign'd,    20
    And Faustus' custom is not to deny
    The just requests of those that wish him well,
    You shall behold that peerless dame of Greece,
    No otherways for pomp and majesty
    Than when Sir Paris cross'd the seas with her
    And brought the spoils to rich Dardania.
    Be silent, then, for danger is in words.

30 pursu'd: *fought to avenge*.
31 ten years' war: *the siege of Troy*.
   rape: *abduction*.
32 passeth all compare: *exceeds all comparison*.

40 bereave: *rob*.

42 persever: *continue*.
43–44 Yet ... nature: *You still have a soul that is worthy of love, if sin does not by habit become natural to you*.

48 exhortation: *urgent advice; warning*.

51 envy of: *ill will towards*.

54 Checking: *rebuking; reproving*.

57 his right: *its rights*.

*Music sounds.* MEPHOSTOPHILIS *brings in* HELEN; *she passeth over the stage.*

1 SCHOLAR  Too simple is my wit to tell her praise
  Whom all the world admires for majesty.
3 SCHOLAR  No marvel though the angry Greeks pursu'd     30
  With ten years' war the rape of such a queen,
  Whose heavenly beauty passeth all compare.
1 SCHOLAR  Since we have seen the pride of nature's works
  And only paragon of excellence,
  Let us depart, and for this glorious deed
  Happy and blest be Faustus evermore.
FAUSTUS  Gentlemen, farewell; the same wish I to you.
*Exeunt* Scholars.
*Enter an* OLD MAN.
OLD MAN  O gentle Faustus, leave this damned art,
  This magic, that will charm thy soul to hell
  And quite bereave thee of salvation.     40
  Though thou hast now offended like a man,
  Do not persever in it like a devil.
  Yet, yet, thou hast an amiable soul,
  If sin by custom grow not into nature:
  Then, Faustus, will repentance come too late,
  Then thou art banish'd from the sight of heaven;
  No mortal can express the pains of hell.
  It may be this my exhortation
  Seems harsh and all unpleasant; let it not,
  For, gentle son, I speak it not in wrath     50
  Or envy of thee, but in tender love
  And pity of thy future misery;
  And so have hope that this my kind rebuke,
  Checking thy body, may amend thy soul.
FAUSTUS  Where art thou, Faustus? wretch, what hast thou
    done?
  Damn'd art thou, Faustus, damn'd; despair and die!
MEPHOSTOPHILIS *gives him a dagger.*
  Hell claims his right and with a roaring voice

59 do thee right: *pay you your due.*
60 stay: *stop.*
61 hovers: *who hovers.*
62 vial: *phial; container for liquids.*

69 hapless: *unlucky.*

71 I do despair: *I am unable to believe that God will be merciful.*
72 strives: *struggles.*

76 Revolt: *return (to Lucifer).*
   in piecemeal: *into pieces.*
77 I do repent: *ironically, Faustus's repentance is now offered to Lucifer.*

83 drift: *drifting away from allegiance; delay.*

85 durst: *dared.*

Says, 'Faustus, come; thine hour is almost come';
And Faustus now will come to do thee right.

[FAUSTUS *goes to use the dagger.*]

OLD MAN  O, stay, good Faustus, stay thy desperate steps!  60
    I see an angel hovers o'er thy head
    And with a vial full of precious grace
    Offers to pour the same into thy soul:
    Then call for mercy, and avoid despair.

FAUSTUS  O friend, I feel
    Thy words to comfort my distressed soul.
    Leave me awhile to ponder on my sins.

OLD MAN  Faustus, I leave thee, but with grief of heart,
    Fearing the enemy of thy hapless soul.

*Exit.*

FAUSTUS  Accursed Faustus, where is mercy now?  70
    I do repent, and yet I do despair;
    Hell strives with grace for conquest in my breast.
    What shall I do to shun the snares of death?

MEPHOSTOPHILIS  Thou traitor, Faustus, I arrest thy soul
    For disobedience to my sovereign lord:
    Revolt, or I'll in piecemeal tear thy flesh.

FAUSTUS  I do repent I e'er offended him.
    Sweet Mephostophilis, entreat thy lord
    To pardon my unjust presumption,
    And with my blood again I will confirm  80
    The former vow I made to Lucifer.

MEPHOSTOPHILIS  Do it, then, Faustus, with unfeigned
    heart,
    Lest greater dangers do attend thy drift.

FAUSTUS  Torment, sweet friend, that base and aged man
    That durst dissuade me from thy Lucifer,
    With greatest torment that our hell affords.

MEPHOSTOPHILIS  His faith is great; I cannot touch his
    soul;
    But what I may afflict his body with
    I will attempt, which is but little worth.

91 glut: *satisfy.*

92 unto my paramour: *as my mistress.*

94 clear: *completely.*

99 launch'd a thousand ships: *that is, caused a thousand Greek ships to be launched for the siege of Troy. This echoes a phrase in* Tamburlaine, Part 2, *an earlier play by Marlowe:* 'Helen, whose beauty summoned Greece to arms,/ And drew a thousand ships to Tenedos'.

100 topless: *immeasurably high.*
   Ilium: *Troy.*

101 make me immortal with a kiss: *this repeats a phrase from what was probably Marlowe's first play,* Dido, Queen of Carthage.

103 again: *back.*

107 sack'd: *captured; pillage.*

108 I will combat with weak Menelaus: *Homer's* Iliad *describes how Helen's husband, Menelaus, would have defeated Paris in single combat, had not the goddess Aphrodite intervened. The word 'weak' is therefore rather unfair.*

109 wear thy colours: *like a mediaeval knight.*
   plumed crest: *feathered helmet.*

110 Achilles: *the great Greek warrior. He was killed by Paris, who shot an arrow that struck his only vulnerable point: his heel.*

115 Semele: *in Greek legend, Semele asked Zeus to appear to her in divine splendour. When he did so she was consumed by the lightning which accompanied him.*

116 the monarch of the sky: *the sun-god. Faustus is describing the beauty of the reflection of sunlight on water.*

117 Arethusa: *the nymph of the fountain of Arethusa, on the island of Ortygia.*
   azur'd: *blue.*

121 tribunal: *judgement.*

FAUSTUS One thing, good servant, let me crave of thee          90
    To glut the longing of my heart's desire:
    That I may have unto my paramour
    That heavenly Helen which I saw of late,
    Whose sweet embraces may extinguish clear
    Those thoughts that do dissuade me from my vow,
    And keep mine oath I made to Lucifer.
MEPHOSTOPHILIS This or what else my Faustus shall desire
    Shall be perform'd in twinkling of an eye.
*Enter* HELEN *again, passing over between two* Cupids.
FAUSTUS Was this the face that launch'd a thousand ships
    And burnt the topless towers of Ilium?          100
    Sweet Helen, make me immortal with a kiss.
    Her lips suck forth my soul: see where it flies!
    Come, Helen, come, give me my soul again.
    Here will I dwell, for heaven is in these lips,
    And all is dross that is not Helena.
*Enter* Old Man.
    I will be Paris, and for love of thee
    Instead of Troy shall Wittenberg be sack'd,
    And I will combat with weak Menelaus
    And wear thy colours on my plumed crest,
    Yea, I will wound Achilles in the heel          110
    And then return to Helen for a kiss.
    O, thou art fairer than the evening's air
    Clad in the beauty of a thousand stars,
    Brighter art thou than flaming Jupiter
    When he appear'd to hapless Semele,
    More lovely than the monarch of the sky
    In wanton Arethusa's azur'd arms,
    And none but thou shalt be my paramour.
*Exeunt* [FAUSTUS, HELEN, *and the* Cupids].
OLD MAN Accursed Faustus, miserable man,
    That from thy soul exclud'st the grace of heaven          120
    And flies the throne of his tribunal seat!
*Enter the* DEVILS.

122 sift: *test*.
   pride: *display of power*.
123 try: *test*.
125 smiles: *smile*.
126 At your repulse: *at how you are repelled*.
   state: *power*.

1 Dis: *alternative name for Pluto, the god of the underworld. Here, it is applied to the underworld itself.*

10 demean: *conduct*.

12 Fond: *foolish*.

16 sauc'd with: *paid for dearly with*.

Satan begins to sift me with his pride:
As in this furnace God shall try my faith,
My faith, vile hell, shall triumph over thee.
Ambitious fiends, see how the heavens smiles
At your repulse and laughs your state to scorn!
Hence, hell! for hence I fly unto my God.

*Exeunt.*


## Scene two

*Thunder. Enter* LUCIFER, BEELZEBUB, *and* MEPHOSTOPHILIS [*above*].

LUCIFER  Thus from infernal Dis do we ascend
　　To view the subjects of our monarchy,
　　Those souls which sin seals the black sons of hell,
　　'Mong which as chief, Faustus, we come to thee,
　　Bringing with us lasting damnation
　　To wait upon thy soul; the time is come
　　Which makes it forfeit.

MEPHOSTOPHILIS　　　　　　　　And this gloomy night
　　Here in this room will wretched Faustus be.

BEELZEBUB  And here we'll stay
　　To mark him how he doth demean himself.　　　　　　10

MEPHOSTOPHILIS  How should he but in desperate lunacy?
　　Fond worldling, now his heart-blood dries with grief,
　　His conscience kills it, and his labouring brain
　　Begets a world of idle fantasies
　　To overreach the devil; but all in vain:
　　His store of pleasures must be sauc'd with pain.
　　He and his servant Wagner are at hand,
　　Both come from drawing Faustus' latest will.
　　See where they come.

*Enter* FAUSTUS *and* WAGNER.

FAUSTUS  Say, Wagner, thou hast perus'd my will:　　　　20
　　How dost thou like it?

WAGNER　　　　　　　　　Sir, so wondrous well

24 Gramercies: *thank you.*

28 chamber-fellow: *student sharing the same room.*

31 imports: *means.*

36 surfeit: *illness caused by over-eating or excessive drinking.*

42 serpent: *see* Genesis III: 1–15.

As in all humble duty I do yield
My life and lasting service for your love.
*Enter the* SCHOLARS.
FAUSTUS Gramercies, Wagner. Welcome, gentlemen.
[*Exit* WAGNER.]
1 SCHOLAR Now, worthy Faustus, methinks your looks are
    changed.
FAUSTUS Ah, gentlemen!
2 SCHOLAR What ails Faustus?
FAUSTUS Ah, my sweet chamber-fellow, had I lived with
    thee, then had I lived still, but now must die eternally.
    Look, sirs, comes he not? comes he not?                    30
1 SCHOLAR O my dear Faustus, what imports this fear?
2 SCHOLAR Is all our pleasure turned to melancholy?
3 SCHOLAR He is not well with being over-solitary.
2 SCHOLAR If it be so, we'll have physicians, and Faustus
    shall be cured.
3 SCHOLAR 'Tis but a surfeit, sir; fear nothing.
FAUSTUS A surfeit of deadly sin, that hath damned both
    body and soul.
2 SCHOLAR Yet, Faustus, look up to heaven and remember
    God's mercy is infinite.                                   40
FAUSTUS But Faustus' offence can ne'er be pardoned: the
    serpent that tempted Eve may be saved, but not Faus-
    tus. Ah, gentlemen, hear me with patience, and tremble
    not at my speeches. Though my heart pants and quivers
    to remember that I have been a student here these thir-
    ty years, O, would I had never seen Wittenberg, never
    read book! and what wonders I have done all Germany
    can witness, yea, all the world, for which Faustus hath
    lost both Germany and the world, yea, heaven itself –
    heaven, the seat of God, the throne of the blessed, the    50
    kingdom of joy – and must remain in hell for ever. Hell,
    ah, hell for ever! Sweet friends, what shall become of
    Faustus, being in hell for ever?
3 SCHOLAR Yet, Faustus, call on God.

55 abjured: *rejected*.

58 stays: *stops*.

63 cunning: *skill*.

66 vain: *empty*.
67 felicity: *happiness*.
   bill: *deed*.

72–73 the devil ... named God: *see Act II, Scene II, line 83 and Act V, Scene I, line 76*.
74 gave ear: *listened*.

80 let us: *let us go*.

FAUSTUS On God, whom Faustus hath abjured? on God, whom Faustus hath blasphemed? Ah, my God, I would weep, but the devil draws in my tears. Gush forth blood, instead of tears, yea, life and soul! O, he stays my tongue! I would lift up my hands, but see, they hold them, they hold them.   60

ALL Who, Faustus?

FAUSTUS Why, Lucifer and Mephostophilis. Ah, gentlemen, I gave them my soul for my cunning.

ALL God forbid!

FAUSTUS God forbade it, indeed; but Faustus hath done it. For the vain pleasure of four-and-twenty years hath Faustus lost eternal joy and felicity. I writ them a bill with mine own blood: the date is expired, this is the time, and he will fetch me.

1 SCHOLAR Why did not Faustus tell us of this before, that   70 divines might have prayed for thee?

FAUSTUS Oft have I thought to have done so; but the devil threatened to tear me in pieces if I named God, to fetch me body and soul if I once gave ear to divinity; and now 'tis too late. Gentlemen, away, lest you perish with me!

2 SCHOLAR O, what may we do to save Faustus?

FAUSTUS Talk not of me, but save yourselves and depart.

3 SCHOLAR God will strengthen me. I will stay with Faustus.

1 SCHOLAR Tempt not God, sweet friend; but let us into   80 the next room and there pray for him.

FAUSTUS Ay, pray for me, pray for me; and, what noise soever ye hear, come not unto me, for nothing can rescue me.

2 SCHOLAR Pray thou, and we will pray, that God may have mercy upon thee.

FAUSTUS Gentlemen, farewell. If I live till morning, I'll visit you; if not, Faustus is gone to hell.

ALL Faustus, farewell.

*Exeunt* Scholars.

94 Hath: *which has*.

97 Damn'd up: *blocked*.

98 To view the scriptures: *for instance, to read the texts quoted in Act I, Scene I, lines 39–41. Mephostophilis is explaining that he was responsible for ensuring that Faustus did not read further in each case.*

105 perpetually: *this word is to recur hauntingly in line 142.*

108 store: *plenty*.

s.d. the throne: *this was lowered by means of cords and pulleys, and represents the seat that Faustus might have occupied in heaven.*

111 affected: *chosen*.

114 hadst sit: *would have sat*.

MEPHOSTOPHILIS Ay, Faustus, now thou hast no hope of   90
    heaven;
  Therefore despair, think only upon hell,
  For that must be thy mansion, there to dwell.
FAUSTUS O thou bewitching fiend, 'twas thy temptation
  Hath robb'd me of eternal happiness.
MEPHOSTOPHILIS I do confess it, Faustus, and rejoice.
  'Twas I that, when thou wert i' the way to heaven,
  Damm'd up thy passage; when thou took'st the book
  To view the scriptures, then I turn'd the leaves
  And led thine eye.
  What, weep'st thou? 'tis too late, despair, farewell!   100
  Fools that will laugh on earth must weep in hell.
*Exit.*
*Enter the* GOOD ANGEL *and the* BAD ANGEL *at several doors.*
GOOD ANGEL O Faustus, if thou hadst given ear to me,
  Innumerable joys had follow'd thee;
  But thou didst love the world.
BAD ANGEL                 Gave ear to me,
  And now must taste hell's pains perpetually.
GOOD ANGEL O, what will all thy riches, pleasures, pomps
  Avail thee now?
BAD ANGEL            Nothing but vex thee more,
  To want in hell, that had on earth such store.
*Music while the throne descends.*
GOOD ANGEL O, thou hast lost celestial happiness,
  Pleasures unspeakable, bliss without end.   110
  Hadst thou affected sweet divinity,
  Hell or the devil had had no power on thee.
  Hadst thou kept on that way, Faustus, behold
  In what resplendent glory thou hadst sit
  In yonder throne, like those bright shining saints,
  And triumph'd over hell; that hast thou lost.
  And now, poor soul, must thy good angel leave thee;
  The jaws of hell are open to receive thee.
*Exit.*

s.d.  discovered: *the throne is raised, and hell is revealed by the drawing of a curtain.*

123  quarters: *of human bodies.*
124  That: *this refers back to 'quarters'.*

126  sops: *ordinary 'sops' were pieces of bread or cake soaked in beer or wine.*

132  smart: *pain; sting.*

134  anon: *presently.*

141  nature's eye: *sun.*
143  natural day: *mere day.*
145  O lente ... equi!: (Latin) *'Gallop slowly, slowly, you horses of the night.' The quotation is from Ovid's* Amores, *which Marlowe had translated. The context is ironic, for the words are those of a lover wishing to prolong the night in his mistress's arms.*
146  still: *always; unceasingly.*
149  streams: *this word recalls ironically 'Why streams it not?' in Act II, Scene I, line 66.*

*Hell is discovered.*

BAD ANGEL  Now, Faustus, let thine eyes with horror stare
　　Into that vast perpetual torture-house.　　　　　　　　　120
　　There are the furies, tossing damned souls
　　On burning forks; their bodies boil in lead:
　　There are live quarters broiling on the coals,
　　That ne'er can die: this ever-burning chair
　　Is for o'er-tortur'd souls to rest them in:
　　These that are fed with sops of flaming fire
　　Were gluttons and lov'd only delicates
　　And laugh'd to see the poor starve at their gates.
　　But yet all these are nothing; thou shalt see
　　Ten thousand tortures that more horrid be.　　　　　　　130

FAUSTUS  O, I have seen enough to torture me.

BAD ANGEL  Nay, thou must feel them, taste the smart of
　　　　all:
　　He that loves pleasure must for pleasure fall:
　　And so I leave thee, Faustus, till anon;
　　Then wilt thou tumble in confusion.

*Exit.*

*The clock strikes eleven.*

FAUSTUS  Ah, Faustus,
　　Now hast thou but one bare hour to live,
　　And then thou must be damn'd perpetually.
　　Stand still, you ever-moving spheres of heaven,
　　That time may cease, and midnight never come;　　　140
　　Fair nature's eye, rise, rise again, and make
　　Perpetual day; or let this hour be but
　　A year, a month, a week, a natural day,
　　That Faustus may repent and save his soul.
　　*O lente lente currite noctis equi!*
　　The stars move still, time runs, the clock will strike,
　　The devil will come, and Faustus must be damn'd.
　　O, I'll leap up to my God! Who pulls me down?
　　See, see where Christ's blood streams in the firmament!

150 One drop ... soul: *reference to the Christian doctrine of redemption, whereby the blood shed by Christ on the cross can continue to save man from hell if he repents his sins.*

153 Where is it now?: *the vision of Christ's blood is now gone, because of the invocation to Lucifer.*

154 ireful: *angry.*

155 Mountains and hills ... on me: *compare* Hosea, X: 8 *'And they shall say to the mountains, Cover us; and to the hills, Fall on us' and* Revelations VI: 16 *'And said to the mountains and rocks, Fall on us, and hide us from the face of him that sitteth on the throne, and from the wrath of the Lamb.'*

156 heavy wrath: *phrase used by the Good Angel in his very first speech – Act I, Scene I, line 71.*

161 influence: *in astrology, the position of the stars at birth is said to influence the pattern of life. Faustus implores the stars that ordained this fate to suck him up in vapour into a cloud and then in a thunderstorm expel his body. This would leave his purified soul fit for admission to heaven.*

163 labouring: *heavy; swelling.*

s.d. watch: *clock.*

174 limited: *appointed definitively.*

177 Pythagoras' metempsychosis: *Pythagoras was a Greek philosopher and mathematician (540–510 BC). He taught the doctrine of the transmigration of souls, which suggested that the human soul took on another form of life after the death of the body.*

179 Unto: *into.*

182 still: *always; ever.*

One drop would save my soul, half a drop. Ah, my          150
   Christ! –
Rend not my heart for naming of my Christ;
Yet will I call on him. O, spare me, Lucifer! –
Where is it now? 'Tis gone: and see where God
Stretcheth out his arm and bends his ireful brows.
Mountains and hills, come, come, and fall on me,
And hide me from the heavy wrath of God!
No, no:
Then will I headlong run into the earth.
Earth, gape! O, no, it will not harbour me.
You stars that reign'd at my nativity,                     160
Whose influence hath allotted death and hell,
Now draw up Faustus like a foggy mist
Into the entrails of yon labouring cloud,
That, when you vomit forth into the air,
My limbs may issue from your smoky mouths,
So that my soul may but ascend to heaven.
*The watch strikes.*
Ah, half the hour is pass'd: 'twill all be pass'd anon.
O God,
If thou wilt not have mercy on my soul,
Yet for Christ's sake, whose blood hath ransom'd me,       170
Impose some end to my incessant pain;
Let Faustus live in hell a thousand years,
A hundred thousand, and at last be sav'd.
O, no end is limited to damned souls.
Why wert thou not a creature wanting soul?
Or why is this immortal that thou hast?
Ah, Pythagoras' *metempsychosis*, were that true,
This soul should fly from me and I be chang'd
Unto some brutish beast: all beasts are happy,
For when they die                                          180
Their souls are soon dissolv'd in elements;
But mine must live still to be plagu'd in hell.
Curs'd be the parents that engender'd me!

187 quick: *alive*.

193 my books: *here, of magic*.
Ah, Mephostophilis!: *Mephostophilis has returned as one of the devils who are to drag Faustus away.*

9 methought: *it seemed to me*.

15 for: *because*.

No, Faustus, curse thyself, curse Lucifer
That hath depriv'd thee of the joys of heaven.
*The clock striketh twelve.*
    O, it strikes, it strikes! Now, body, turn to air,
Or Lucifer will bear thee quick to hell!
*Thunder and lightning.*
    O soul, be chang'd into little water drops,
And fall into the ocean, ne'er be found.
*Enter* DEVILS.
    My God, my God! Look not so fierce on me!       190
Adders and serpents, let me breathe awhile!
Ugly hell, gape not! Come not, Lucifer;
I'll burn my books! – Ah, Mephostophilis!
*Exeunt with him.* [*Exeunt* LUCIFER *and* BEELZEBUB.]

## Scene three

*Enter the* SCHOLARS.

1 SCHOLAR Come, gentlemen, let us go visit Faustus,
    For such a dreadful night was never seen
    Since first the world's creation did begin;
    Such fearful shrieks and cries were never heard.
    Pray heaven the doctor have escap'd the danger.
2 SCHOLAR O, help us, heaven! see, here are Faustus'
    limbs,
    All torn asunder by the hand of death.
3 SCHOLAR The devils whom Faustus serv'd have torn him
    thus;
    For, 'twixt the hours of twelve and one, methought
    I heard him shriek and call aloud for help,       10
    At which self time the house seem'd all on fire
    With dreadful horror of these damned fiends.
2 SCHOLAR Well, gentlemen, though Faustus' end be such
    As every Christian heart laments to think on,
    Yet, for he was a scholar, once admir'd

16 schools: *universities.*

19 wait upon: *accompany on its way.*
   heavy: *sorrowful.*

For wondrous knowledge in our German schools,
We'll give his mangled limbs due burial;
And all the students, cloth'd in mourning black,
Shall wait upon his heavy funeral.

*Exeunt.*

3 Apollo: *the Greek god of poetry and song. Here he is associated with learning or genius.*
  laurel bough: *the laurel was a mark of distinction given to poets.*
4 sometime: *at one time.*
6 fiendful: *caused by devils.*
7 Only to wonder: *to be content with merely wondering.*
8 forward wits: *advanced thinkers.*

Terminat . . . opus: (Latin) *'The hour ends the day; the author ends his work.' This motto was probably added by the first printer.*

# Epilogue

*Enter* Chorus.

CHORUS Cut is the branch that might have grown full straight,
    And burned is Apollo's laurel bough
    That sometime grew within this learned man.
    Faustus is gone: regard his hellish fall,
    Whose fiendful fortune may exhort the wise
    Only to wonder at unlawful things,
    Whose deepness doth entice such forward wits
    To practise more than heavenly power permits.

[*Exit.*]

*Terminat hora diem; terminat Author opus.*
                 *FINIS.*

# Study questions

1 'A little learning is a dangerous thing.' Is this the message of *Doctor Faustus*?
2 What do the comic scenes contribute to the meaning and effect of *Doctor Faustus*?
3 'The greatness of *Doctor Faustus* lies in the power of its poetry.' Assess the poetry of the play in the light of this comment.
4 How appropriate do you find the Prologue and Epilogue of *Doctor Faustus*?
5 'Tragedy emphasizes the nobility and value of man.' Is *Doctor Faustus* a tragedy in this sense?
6 Analyze the treatment in *Doctor Faustus* of two of the following: blood; fire; magic; food; gold.
7 'Mephostophilis is both more honest and more intelligent than Faustus himself.' Do you agree with this claim?
8 Discuss the presentation of hell in *Doctor Faustus*.
9 How is the relationship between masters and servants handled in *Doctor Faustus*?
10 '*Doctor Faustus* fails to convince its audience that goodness and orthodoxy are attractive.' Do you consider this to be a valid criticism of the play?